DATE DUE

AUG 3 1 2012	

Floristry

A STEP-BY-STEP GUIDE

JUDITH BLACKLOCK AND LESLEY YOUNG

Floristry

A STEP-BY-STEP GUIDE

Published by:

The Flower Press Ltd
3 East Avenue
Bournemouth
BH3 7BW

This First Edition published 2010

Designed by SCW Design www.scw.uk.com

Printed and bound in China by C&C Offset Printing

A CIP catalogue record for this book is available from the British Library.

ISBN -13: 978-0-9552391-5-1

ISBN -10: 0-9552391-5-X

Contents

Introduction

Floristry is a trade to be enjoyed. Nature is constantly providing a diverse supply of materials and so are the growers. Although many flowers and foliage are available for most of the year, seasonal varieties bring a joy and excitement to designs. In this book we have tried to offer designs using both year round staples and delightful seasonal flowers. We suggest alternatives to the plant material shown in the designs so they can be achieved worldwide whatever the season. Tips relating to each design are offered throughout.

Floristry also changes with fashion which keeps it challenging and stimulating. Floral designers need to keep ahead with trends in interiors, textiles, clothing and in other areas where flowers are used to accessorise. Florists also deal with emotion - celebrating through flowers all the key events in life, including: births, christenings, weddings, birthdays, anniversaries and commemorating deaths.

If you are a newcomer to floristry it is vital to learn the essential building blocks of design. We have worked together to provide thorough yet simple step-by-step guides that will enable you to re-create the designs without stress. We hope this book provides you with the basis for your chosen trade and craft.

Judith Blacklock and Lesley Young

OASIS

chapter 1

Tools of the trade

There is a wealth of both obvious and unexpected items available to the florist.

Tools and equipment will build up with time and experience but it makes sense to start with the essentials. None of the individual items mentioned on the following pages are expensive. Ideally you should purchase some kind of toolbox, from any hardware retailer, in which they can be stored and carried.

In terms of sourcing, most tools are specialist items. Some can be purchased from large garden centres, but most florist shops are understandably reluctant to sell the tools of their trade or simply do not have the space to stock them. It is therefore best to go to a florists' wholesaler. These are usually made accessible via a floristry course. There is often a minimum purchase requirement, though these are seldom prohibitive.

The list overleaf will enable the beginner to create the designs featured in this book - and more.

Tool box contents

1. **Florists' knife** – this is a small, lightweight but sharp knife capable of cutting both soft and semi-woody stems at a sharp angle to expose the maximum amount of cells for the easy uptake of water.

2. **Floristry scissors** – these are strong, specialist scissors which have the facility to cut wire as well as soft and semi-woody stems. You should also have a separate pair of sharp scissors for cutting ribbon.

3. **Secateurs** – a must for cutting harder, woodier stems such as shrubby foliage and roses. There are various types available from garden centres and hardware stores but a standard pair for cutting stems will suffice.

4. **Wire cutters or pliers** – you may prefer to ease the strain on floristry scissors and use these to cut stub wires or chicken wire.

5. **Rose stripper by OASIS®** – a yellow round plastic pad, which is easy to hold and, when drawn firmly down a stem, removes leaves and thorns with ease.

6. **Stub wires** – you will need a range of gauges including 0.28 mm, 0.32 mm, 0.56 mm, 0.71 mm and 0.90 mm. Sometimes 1.50 mm is needed for heavier mechanics.

7. **Reel wires** – there are two types: **functional** and **decorative**.

   Functional reel wires are needed in two main gauges - 0.56 mm, which is ideal for attaching moss to a wire frame (it is often known as 'mossing' wire), and a lighter 0.32 mm gauge for wired wedding designs.

   In recent years, **decorative** wires have grown immensely popular and are now available in a huge range of lovely colours from subtle rose pink to the boldest electric blue. Even basic toolboxes should stock several of these. The smooth decorative wires are mostly available in a 0.46 mm gauge, or occasionally a much finer 0.28 mm gauge. There is also the slightly wavy 'bullion' wire in a 0.32 mm gauge, which adds texture to designs.

8. **Twine** – mainly used for tying stems in handtieds, or twigs in structures. It can, however, cut into delicate stems so a softer polypropylene twine is best.

9. **Cold glue** – now used in so many designs, particularly those for adornment, and for attaching flower heads and leaves to foundations. Unlike hot glue, it does not stain or burn the plant material. It is best left for a minute prior to attachment so that it becomes slightly tacky and thus adheres more effectively.

10. **Glue gun** – this is ideal for more heavy-duty gluing and sets almost immediately. White sticks of glue are placed into the rear nozzle of the gun, which is then plugged into the power socket. When the trigger is pulled, heated glue is extruded from the nozzle. The glue sets transparent, but is best used for non-fresh materials because it leaves burn marks on fresh plant material. It is also visible on transparent materials such as skeletonised leaves. Take care not to let hot glue drip onto skin, because it will burn.

11. **Pot tape** – used to anchor florists' foam into containers. It is available in dark green and in two widths. The wider one is best for larger designs where more strength is needed.

12. **Stem tape** – used to conceal wires for camouflage and also to cover sharp ends. Parafilm® has a plastic texture and is slightly more expensive but goes twice as far as Stemtex® which has a papery texture. It should be stretched until transparent for best use. Stem tape is widely available in green, brown and white, though Stemtex® is also produced in some other colours such as pink and lilac.

13. **Double-sided sticky tape** – good for attaching leaves onto a plastic

or glass bowl or ribbon onto a plastic bouquet handle. It can be easier to use than cold glue, as it is less messy.

14. **Stapler –** used for pleating ribbon to be used as edging on funeral tributes and for manipulating foliage. Buy one that is easy to hold.

15. **Florists' fix –** this looks a little like green Blu-Tack® but is much stickier. It has a range of fixing uses, such as adhering plastic frog prongs (foam holders) to the bases of containers. It is difficult to remove once used.

16. **Paper-covered wire / bind wire –** can be used to bind stems in tied designs and is particularly good for heavier stems. It has a range of other uses such as binding twig structures. Available in thin and thicker reels and in dark green, lime green, light brown, black, gold, yellow and pink.

17. **Pins –** can be functional silver types (for pinning a ribbon edging onto a funeral tribute), or decorative with a coloured head. They are both available in varying lengths. These are good for attaching buttonholes and corsages to lapels and ribbon onto the stems of handtieds.
There are also black steel pins. German pins (mossing pins) are more functional and are useful for securing materials into designs.

18. **Measuring tape –** for measuring space allocation for designs and head sizes for headdresses.

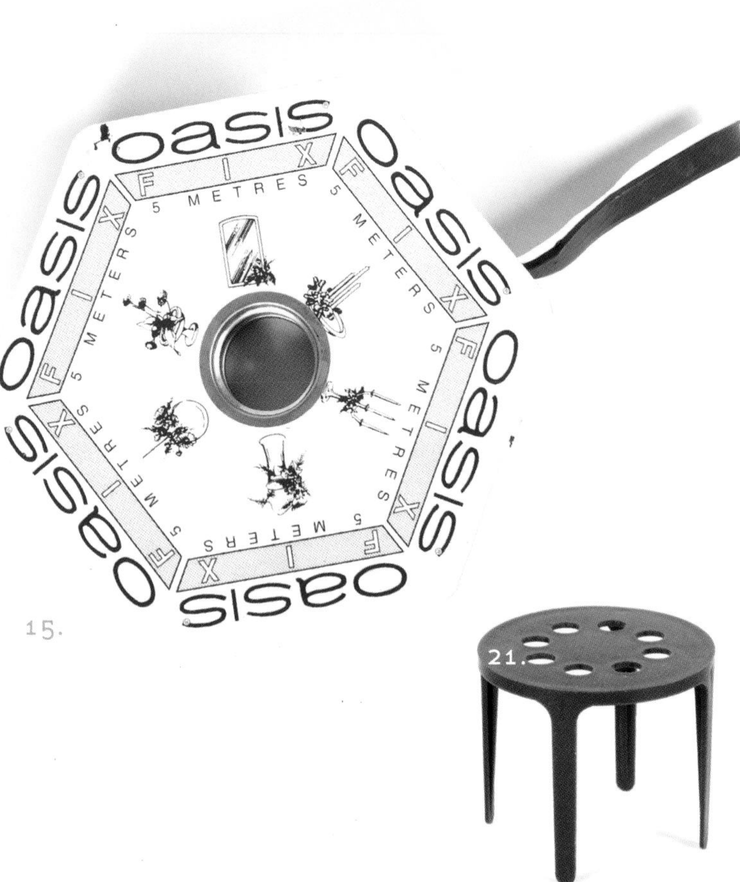

15.

21.

19. **Ribbons –** ideally a selection of the following:

wired-edge ribbon – though there are many ribbons on the market, a wired-edged ribbon in a neutral colour such as green will make a perfect bow every time.

polypropylene ribbon – best for ribbon pleating on funeral tributes as it is water repellent. It is inexpensive.

satin ribbon – used for covering handles on plastic bouquet holders and covering the stem on a bridal handtied.

20. **Pin holders –** coming back into fashion because they are ideal for spring flowers. When placed in the base of a shallow container, stems are inserted into the needle-like protrusions to stabilise.

21. **Frog –** a round plastic disc with four thin protrusions onto which foam may be anchored.

22. **Leaf wipes / leaf shine spray –** improves the cleanliness and surface texture of most broad leaves. The wipes will clean a dirty leaf though not give much shine, whilst the spray will leave a high gloss.

Other equipment

1. **Florists' foam –** arguably one of the best known and widely used florist sundries. It has become the essential medium for securing stems and is often known by the brand name of OASIS®. The most common shape is a green brick, which soaks up water in approximately 50 seconds. There are also many other shapes.

   Floral foam is also produced in a dry grey form, which will not soak up water and is for use with dried and artificial flowers.

2. **Candle cup –** this small plastic cup holds a cylinder of foam and is designed to be placed into a candleholder on a candelabra.

3. **Plastic tray –** used for a range of standard arrangements such as those for buffet tables, or even small coffin sprays for funerals. They are available in three lengths (taking one, two or three bricks of foam) in black or green plastic.

4. **Plastic shovels –** originally designed for funeral work, but they can also be used for hanging wall designs.

5. **Garland cages –** plastic oblong cages used to encase pre-cut pieces of foam. Primarily used for garlands.

6. **Plastic bowls –** these take a large quantity of foam. They are deeper than plastic trays (3) so are good for larger arrangements such as pedestals.

7. **Candle holders –** these will hold a standard sized candle and the pointed end is then inserted into foam. However, they are not widely used because wire hairpins can be taped to the base of the candle to secure into foam instead.

8. **Le Klip® –** these small spheres of foam enclosed in a green plastic cage have a clip on the back, which can be placed over some church pew ends. They are also used for other hanging designs.

9. **Le Bump® –** a small, rounded piece of foam encased in a plastic green cage. It has a metal spring on the underside, which secures it when screwed onto a foam base. It is frequently used to create a spray on top of a based funeral tribute.

10. **Sphere –** a rounded piece of foam used for a wide range of designs – in this book used for a bridesmaid's pomander and bridal orb.

11. **Bouquet holders –** used for creating handheld posies and bridal bouquets. Bouquet holders have a plastic handle with a section of wet or dry floral foam encased on top, into which stems are inserted. The holders come in various sizes and shapes and they are manufactured by leading companies, OASIS® and Val Spicer and others.

12. **Chicken wire –** this is available in several different gauges and finishes (including green and silvery grey). Generally the lighter the gauge, the more expensive. It also has different hole sizes, which is an important consideration. It is used:

- for the protection of foam so that it will not crumble when being used in large-scale pedestal designs.
- as a support mechanic. In this case, select wire with larger holes, which is more pliable and allows stems to be inserted easily.
- crumpled in a container holding water – the best medium for bulb flowers.

13. **Wire wreath frame –** metal rings available in a range of sizes from 25 cm (10 in) up to 40 cm (16 in) in diameter. Frames also come in cross, chaplet and heart shapes - though these are less widely used. The rings are now mainly used to make door wreaths at Christmas.

14. **Wrapping materials –** there are many kinds of wrapping materials such as clear Cellophane and brown paper. When either is combined with coloured tissue paper, they are popular for wrapping flowers. There are many other materials with a distinctly more fabric-like texture such as 'Fabtex'.

15. **Magnets –** used to attach corsages to clothing. Always check that the recipient is not fitted with a pacemaker. They will also affect some watches.

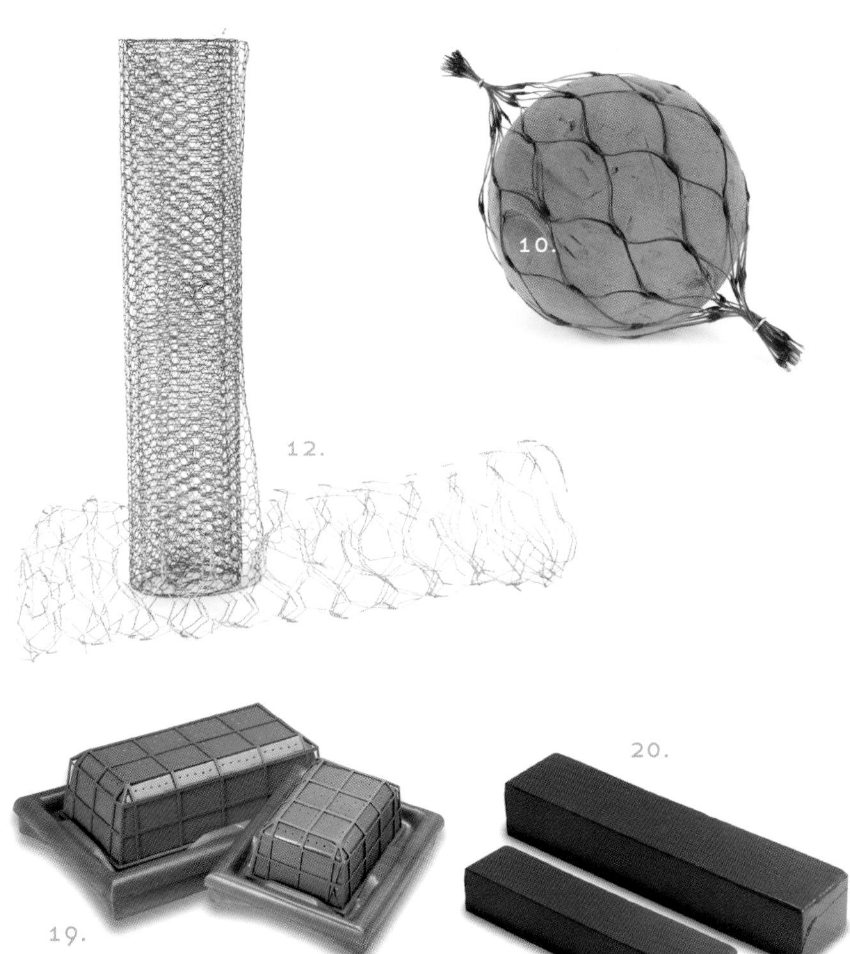

16. **Plastic wire holders –** these are thin, plastic tubes, which are useful in toolboxes to keep wires tidy and easily accessible.

17. **T-bar –** a small, plastic base in the shape of a 'T' with a safety pin on the back to which you can attach the handle of a corsage.

18. **Cable ties –** plastic electricians' ties provide a strong support and connection between different elements of a design.

19. **OASIS® Floral Foam Casket Saddles** – these are available in the USA to fit on the funeral casket. They consist of OASIS® foam wrapped in green Polyfilm to hold in moisture. The wrapped foam is covered with a cage that supports the flowers during transport and display. The sturdy moulded urethane base has scratch-guard rubber strips and a deep reservoir for water.

20. **OASIS® Floral Foam RAQUETTES® Holder –** these are used for many occasions where a long horizontal or vertical design is required. The foam is wrapped in perforated green ply film which holds the moisture. It is available in different lengths. The RAQUETTE has a rigid plastic base with two drilled holes. It is commonly used for sympathy work on the casket/coffin.

chapter 2

The elements and principles of design

For those of you who are relatively new to the application of the elements and principles of design, a useful way to distinguish between the two is to remember that an element is something that occurs naturally, whereas principles are something that we apply to achieve a certain effect.

Form, colour, texture and space are the four elements of design and a quick way to remember them is:

Florists **C**ut **T**rees and **S**hrubs

Balance, contrast, dominance, harmony, proportion, rhythm and scale are the principles. Although it is useful to memorize these in alphabetical order, they are all equally important. Over time and with repetition, the application of these principles will become instinctive. They will not necessarily all apply to any one design and some will predominate more than others, but they will remain your essential building blocks of design.

Elements of design in floristry

Form

In floristry, form refers to the shape of the plant materials being used and the arrangement as a whole. Often the word shape is used instead of form, but shape should be considered as two-dimensional. Form, however, is regarded as having depth as well as height and width, and is therefore three-dimensional.

Plant materials have traditionally been categorised as mass, spike and transitional.

Mass – the bold, round forms that provide dominance and impact in designs. These include sunflowers (*Helianthus*), *Allium*, open roses and *Gerbera*.

There are other bold flowers that would fit this category, but which are not always round such as bird-of-paradise (*Strelitzia*).

Spike – dogwood (*Cornus*), bulrushes, *Delphinium*, *Liatris* and *Aconitum* are all good examples of linear materials. The linear, architectural look of the *Mahonia japonica*, with its perfect leaf repetition, gives a strong vertical line and would therefore also be classed as a spike or linear form.

Transitional – in-between or filler flowers, such as lisianthus (*Eustoma*), *Alstroemeria*, and September flower (*Aster*). These are essential in mixed designs because they provide a visual link between the spike and mass forms.

Colour

It was Sir Isaac Newton who, in 1666, discovered the colour spectrum by passing a beam of light through a prism, which separated it into seven colours: red, orange, yellow, green, blue, indigo (or blue-violet) and violet.

Colour - or hue as it is referred in colour terms - is a sensation conveyed through our eyes via light waves.

Primary Colours

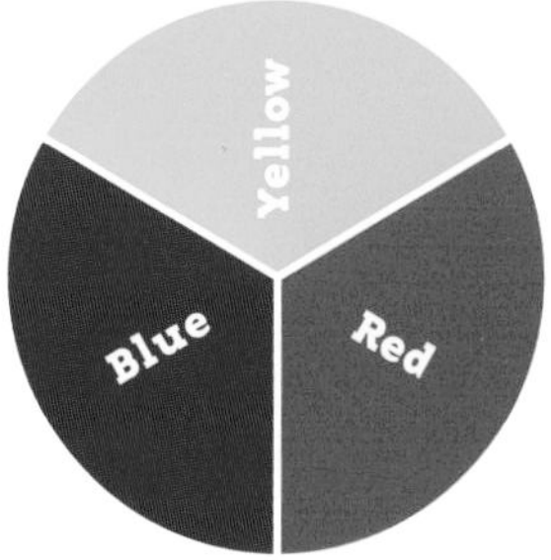

These three colours cannot be created by mixing other colours together. It is by mixing these primaries that all other colours are produced. On the colour wheel, the primary colours are placed apart equidistantly.

Secondary Colours

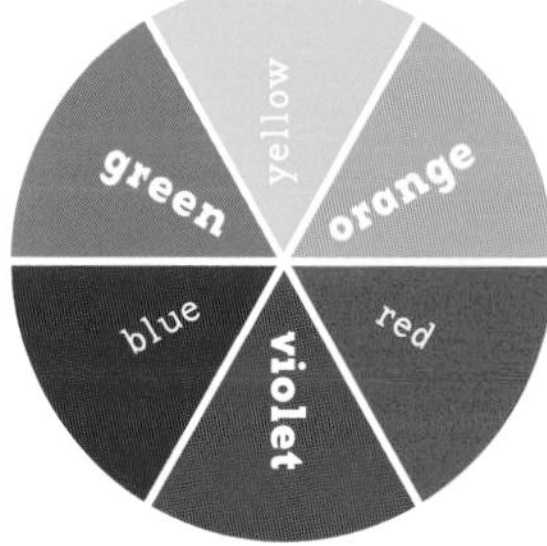

These three colours are obtained by mixing two primaries together.

Primaries		Secondary
Yellow + red	=	orange
Red + blue	=	violet
Blue + yellow	=	green

Tertiary Colours

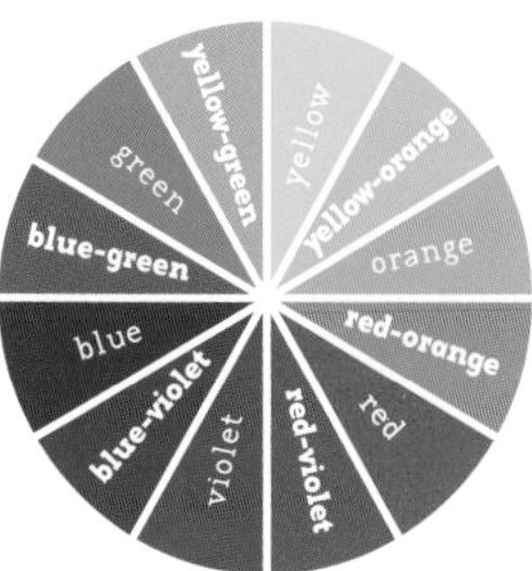

These six colours are obtained by mixing one primary colour with its neighbouring secondary colour.

Primary		Secondary		Tertiary
Yellow	+	orange	=	yellow-orange
Red	+	orange	=	red-orange
Red	+	violet	=	red-violet
Blue	+	violet	=	blue-violet
Blue	+	green	=	blue-green
Yellow	+	green	=	yellow-green

When naming the double-barrelled tertiary colours, the primary colour goes first.

Neutral or achromatic colours

These are black, grey and white. They are not seen in the colour spectrum (or rainbow) and are not on the colour wheel as individual colours. In fact, the term achromatic means absence of colour.

Neutral colours enhance but never dominate, making them a good choice for backgrounds, containers, bases and drapes.

It is the addition of these neutral colours to the pure hues that gives the huge range of colours that we see in existence all around us – whether in nature, paints or textiles.

Addition of **white** to a hue	= a **tint**
Addition of **grey** to a hue	= a **tone**
Addition of **black** to a hue	= a **shade**

We therefore get tints, tones and shades of each basic hue. The colour range is huge and in the case of yellow, for example, this can stretch from the palest cream (with the addition of white) to the earthiest ochre (the addition of black). Red washed out with a generous tint of white will give the palest oyster pink, but darkened with black will give crimson.

Neutralised colours

In reality, there are off-whites, tinted greys, and whitish beiges that are useful alternatives to pure white, grey and black. These are termed neutralised colours and are found in natural materials - such as driftwood, straw or stone - and man-made ones, such as metals, concrete and glass. They have a very weak chroma and can, of course, be a perfect backdrop for small, brilliant areas of colour.

Advancing and receding colours

Some colours advance and are easily noticed. Others recede and are difficult to see in poor light.

The order of visibility, from most visible to least visible, is as follows:

yellow – orange – red – green – blue – purple

Yellow is the most noticeable colour and purple the least. This knowledge helps the florist to select plant material that is suitable for large or small rooms in either poor or bright light. For instance, in a poorly-lit church, the brighter, warmer colours such as yellows, oranges and reds, will be far more noticeable and effective than the darker blues and violets which will recede into the surrounding area.

Colour Harmonies

Monochromatic

Mono means 'one' and this harmony combines the tints, tones and shades of one colour to create a palette of subtle variations. Take blue for instance: from a pure blue will come the palest pastel tint with the addition of white; with the addition of grey, the colour of smoke; and with the addition of black, deepest midnight blue.

This really is a very pleasing and harmonious colour combination and is most traditionally used for weddings because tints, tones and shades have a close relationship with each other.

Analogous / adjacent

This is the use of three or four colours lying next to each other on the colour wheel. A maximum of five colours can be used, but this must not include more than one primary colour. Equally, it is not necessary for a primary colour to be used. This is certainly one of the easier colour schemes for the florist to produce and is very harmonious, because the colours are closely related. Tints, tones and shades of the colours give variety and interest.

An example is: orange, yellow-orange, yellow, yellow-green, and green.

This scheme has yellow as the common link. Similarly, a violet, red-violet, red, red-orange, and orange scheme will have red as its common denominator.

Complementary

This is the use of any two colours lying directly opposite each other on the colour wheel, though any combination of tints, tones and shades can be selected.

Complementary colours containing a primary colour give very striking effects, such as:

- blue and orange
- yellow and violet
- red and green

Polychromatic

This is quite simply the use of many different colours together. A good example of this in floral design is the old Flemish paintings of urns of mixed flowers. It is not a combination much used in floristry today, but these schemes can be very vivid and dramatic. They are more effective if the light and dark values of the hues are varied because too many brilliant colours can cancel each other out. They also look better with a profusion of different flowers.

Texture

Texture is the tactile element of design – its 'touchy feely' nature adds a third dimension to the surface quality of materials. It is the way something feels when you touch it (known as actual texture), but it can also be purely visual. Floristry is mainly concerned with visual texture.

We often describe textures as rough, smooth, shiny, dull, coarse or fine. It is the successful combination and blending of textures that increases depth and visual interest in the design. In floristry terms, juxtaposition - the use of varying textures very close together - gives a pleasing effect.

Textures of containers and accessories

Texture can instantly suggest a look or theme. This is not restricted to fresh plant materials, but extends to containers and accessories. Containers with non-reflective and rough surfaces, such as baskets or unglazed pottery, look natural and informal. Equally, accessories such as driftwood, bark, pods or cones portray a rustic image.

Conversely, smooth and shiny polished surfaces, such as marble, glass or silver, have been symbolic of wealth and high status. They demand the use of appropriate plant materials, such as the elegant crispness of a white *Phalaenopsis* orchid.

Space

Space is much more than simply a gap or a void. Such words conjure up an impression of something that might seem insignificant – a sort of nothingness - and yet space is essential to maximise the impact of anything it surrounds. As one of the four elements of design, it is probably the least referred to - and yet it is as significant as colour, form and texture.

Space defines and enhances form. Because of space, we know objects that would not otherwise be recognisable. Floral designs are three-dimensional objects, like pieces of sculpture, placed in their own area of space. For instance, they could be in the contained space of a niche, or freestanding in open space on a table. Furthermore, the arched area of space forming the niche can be viewed as having a shape all of its own defined as it is by space.

A more significant way for the florist to think about space is to consider how it can be brought into the design itself, so that each component – be it plant material, or accessory – has its own area of space so as not to appear overcrowded.

Space gives a sense of order and tends to eliminate untidiness and clutter. It can also give meaning to an object that would otherwise be unnoticed.

Principles of design in floristry

Balance

In floral design terms, there are two types of balance: visual and actual.

Actual balance

Broadly speaking, this refers to the *physical stability* of the design, which means it should not be at risk of falling over. For instance, a large front-facing design such as a pedestal could be at risk of toppling forward if insufficient weight has been placed at the back, since the majority of plant material is placed at the front and sides. A plastic urn may need to be filled with sand or gravel to support the weight of a large design, particularly if placed on an uneven floor such as in a marquee.

A funeral tribute may feel too heavy if the foam has been over-soaked. Equally, this applies to bridal work; particularly wired bouquets, which should balance on the forefinger by the correct positioning and angling of the materials into the binding point.

Visual Balance

Visual balance means that the design looks stable and not likely to fall over. Visual balance is achieved through the appropriate distribution of the size, form and colour of materials in design work.

- Larger flowers such as *Allium* or sunflowers (*Helianthus*) attract the eye more quickly than smaller ones. Traditionally, smaller bud materials are placed at the outer edges of a design and the larger, bolder flowers - such as peonies and large *Gerbera* - more centrally (though this is not necessarily the case with contemporary design).
- Shinier textures are more eye-catching (because of the light reflection) than dull ones – think of a leaf-shined *Aspidistra* versus a duller salal (*Gaultheria*) leaf.
- Advancing and warmer colours have more emphasis than receding or cooler ones.
- A mass has more power than any other form because it draws the eye in and maintains it.
- Enclosed space, such as an archway, attracts more attention than open space.
- Compact forms have more impact than airy forms (consider sunflowers versus *Gypsophila*).

Contrast

Contrast is the comparison of unlike or opposite qualities and it can be achieved in several ways within floral design. These include the use of horizontal and vertical lines set against each other, such as a vertical grouping of gingers (*Alpinia*) next to a horizontal grouping of *Philodendron* leaves. It may be the juxtaposition of adjacent textures - for example prickly next to smooth - or it may be the use of space next to a solid bed of carnations.

The Society of Floristry defines contrast thus: "to set in opposition in order to show the difference. By placing materials within a design in such a way as to highlight the differences - colour, texture, size, form".

Contrast is essential to prevent an arrangement from being boring.

Dominance

Dominance in a design is important, because there should be *something* that will attract immediate attention and speak, as it were, to the viewer. Other features in the design will then keep that attention by creating a sort of lesser visual path for the eye to roam. It is that initial attention-grabbing feature that is vital. We often refer to this as the focal point, a point of emphasis, or accent area.

Areas of a design must be *unequal* for one to have dominance. Cohesion and unity are more possible when areas are not equally important and are therefore not competing for attention. This emphasis can be achieved by several means – including quantity, size, colour, density, form and position.

Colours with high luminosity, such as yellow and lime green, and light tints (containing a high amount of white) are usually noticed first. These are best used to create dominance in a dark area such as a church. Conversely, darker colours should be placed lower down into the centre of a design as they give visual depth and dominance – particularly when used with shades and tints.

Textures that are shiny with the quality of reflecting light are more dominant than those that are restrained and matt.

Size is another way to achieve a focal point or area of dominance. Larger and more open blooms can be used to draw in the eye. Think of a huge, round *Hydrangea* used at the centre of a large scale design and mixed in with other seasonal and visually lighter companions, such as roses, gladioli or scabious (*Scabiousa*).

Form or shape in unusual, or striking flower forms such as bird-of-paradise flower (*Strelitzia*) or *Heliconia* are often used as focal, dominant or accent flowers due to their unique shape. These tend to look best if used in isolation - with space around them - to enhance their silhouette.

Harmony

Although harmony is widely regarded as a design principle in its own right, it is often best summed up as the final achievement of a successful design when all the principles of design are used well.

We often associate the term harmony with music – when individual sounds from instruments or voices combine with each other to make a pleasing composition. It may be that a theme or mood is being portrayed – formal, sophisticated, tropical – so the designer needs to consider the size, shape, colour and texture of the materials and sundries to create a harmonious composition. In other words, the component parts blend well and evoke the theme. Do they go well together? Are they in tune with each other? Do added accessories enhance the theme?

Containers should harmonise with the materials in the design as well as the background setting and the theme. The size of the design itself and the flowers within it will, of course, influence the choice of container as will a colour. An ill-matched container can easily split the design in two parts.

Flower and foliage size, shape, colour and texture must blend. This does not mean that they should necessarily be the same as this would look too bland, but there should be some cohesion. For instance, tropical flowers tend to be most effective when blended with other tropical flowers, such as *Strelitzia, Heliconia, Leucospermum* and look out of place when mixed with country garden flowers such as *Antirrhinum* or stocks.

Accessories are ideal for depicting themes but are more difficult than any other component to integrate. Care should be taken so that they do not detract in any way from the flowers and they should not dominate. They could simply emulate the same curve of a stem or the texture of a leaf. It is these echoes of repetition that give rhythm and can help to achieve harmony. Repetition of elements is always unifying.

Style and setting – a large room will generally require a large-scale design in order to maintain balance and proportion and ultimately harmony. The period style of the interior may influence the choice of flower materials and container so as to harmonise with its style, as might the patterns and colours of its fabrics and wallpapers.

If the design principles are used well there should be harmony. Repetition of colour, form and texture are the easiest ways to provide links and create harmony. Materials, containers and accessories should be compatible with each other and their setting or occasion.

Proportion

Proportion is the relation of one portion of a display to another – for instance container to arrangement, or arrangement to setting. It refers to quantity or amount, *not* to individual sizes, which is *scale*.

Equal amounts of anything lack interest and widely contrasting amounts do not work. As a general guide, the proportions of three to two are safe. The three refers to the part of the design that is to be dominant; for instance, in a modern handtied, that might be purple *Allium* blooms used with less dominant materials such as *Philodendron* leaves and grasses which would be the two.

It would, however, be a mistake to suggest that we should use an exact mathematical equation (the height of a flower compared to the container, for instance) as the apparent height is dependant on many variables such as colour, texture and form. Eventually, the designer's instinct and judgement in achieving pleasing proportion will be the most reliable.

Rhythm

This refers to the movement of the eye through a design and is needed to prevent it looking boring or monotonous. One of the easiest ways to achieve rhythm is by the use of recession – placing some materials at a lower level in order to create visual depth.

Another way of creating rhythm is the use of curved lines of materials – for instance, in the use of diagonal lines in a coffin spray. Curved plant materials are considered to have more rhythm because the eye does not follow a straight line. Similarly, a repetition of grouped materials provides a visual link such as the repeated groupings of flowers in a Biedermeier handtied.

Contemporary designs often use a more active, sharp rhythm. This is achieved by using material with strong architectural shapes, and using less of it, so that the eye moves distinctly from one form to another.

Scale

Scale is sometimes confused with proportion. To distinguish between the two in a typical floral arrangement, each flower in relation to the container is termed scale - in other words relative dimensions.

Proportion is defined by the *amount* of flowers in relation to the size of the container. Good scale is achieved when various components of a design (be they flowers, containers or accessories) are not too varying in size and therefore link together. If very large materials are used with very small ones, they can be linked together by the addition of a variety of intermediate sizes. These act as 'stepping stones' and provide a more harmonious effect.

Sometimes, though, scale can be deliberately disparate to create impact: the grouping of very small materials can be used alongside much larger ones and still work.

chapter 3

Wiring techniques

Wiring techniques are important in floristry design work. Wires give support and control; they can give anchorage, lengthen stems and bind them together.

Wiring plant material to create small, delicate floral works of art can be very time consuming and difficult to cost. However, the results are exquisite and immensely rewarding for both designer and recipient.

Functional wiring should be as discreet as possible, though with the advent of decorative wires some are used as a design feature. As a general rule, the lightest possible wire gauge - or thickness - should be used, but the material should still have sufficient support. It should have what is referred to as some natural movement and not be too stiff and heavy.

To test whether a flower or foliage is adequately supported, hold the wired stem at the base. If it bends over it is too lightweight, but conversely, if there is no movement at all it is too heavy.

Wired stems should be covered in stem tape to conceal the wire and create a false stem. This also slows the dehydration process: the tape seals in moisture.

Types of wire

Uses

- Supporting a stem such as a *Gerbera* to avoid breakage. In some funeral work, stems may also need extra support due to handling.
- Mounting stems to include in a wired bouquet.
- Stitching small leaves for corsage work, or larger broad leaves in order to manipulate them.

Using stem tape

Stem tape needs to be stretched so finely that it nearly snaps – and if it does, it is easy to start again over the last centimetre of tape.

Wrap the tip of the wire with the fully stretched stem tape so that it is fixed in position. If you are right-handed, twirl the wire with your left hand and with your right pull the tape taught, away and down, at approximately a 130 ° angle.

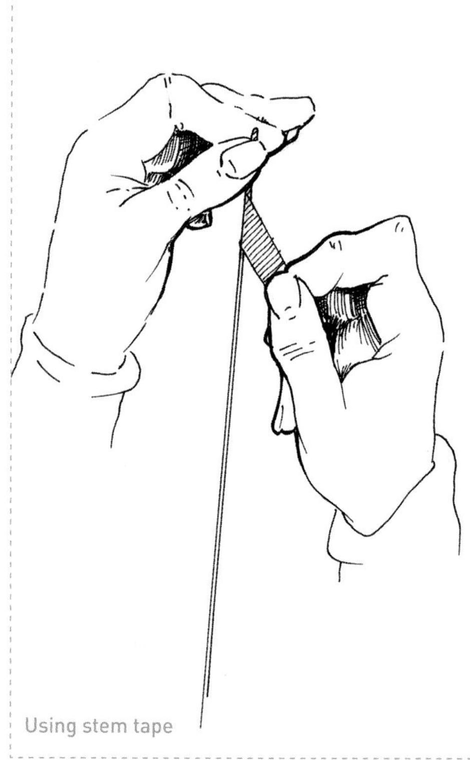

Using stem tape

Wire gauges

mm	swg (standard wire gauge)
1.25	18
1.00	19
0.90	20
0.71	22
0.56	24
0.46	26
0.38	28
0.32	30
0.28	32

Stub wires

These are lengths of wires that are most widely available in either 180 mm or 260 mm lengths, and in a variety of gauges (see table left).

This table shows both metric and imperial measurements but all references will only mention the metric.

Functional stub wires are black annealed, or green coated. There are not many decorative stub wires on the market, though it is possible to find them in red.

Reel wires

These wires tend to be in medium to lighter gauges, ranging from 0.56 mm (such as the 'mossing' reel wire) up to the lighter 0.28 mm, which is best used for binding delicate bridal bouquets. As with the stub wires, the functional reel wires are available coated in a blue / black colour, or green.

Decorative reel wires are also available in a wealth of colours, from bright turquoise and cerise pink to subtler rose pink, or pale lavender. They are available in both smooth, plain wire and wavy wire known as 'bullion.' Another addition in recent years has been paper-covered bind wire. This is also available in different thicknesses and, as well as pale brown and green, it comes in black, gold, pink and lime green.

Uses

- To bind decorative twigs to form structures; it has a natural appearance and an ability to grip well.
- To form decorative bases for corsages and other adornments.
- To embellish decorative accessories such as foliage/floral handbags.
- To support delicate flower stems such as those of lily-of-the-valley (*Convallaria*) and *Freesia*.
- To bind stems in handtieds - though it is best used with harder, woodier stems as it can cut softer ones.

Aluminium wire

This decorative wire is characterised by its pliability and is often referred to as 'bendy' wire. It is thicker than the other decorative reel wires (2 mm gauge) and is sold in shorter lengths - usually of 2 m (6½ ft). Like other decorative wires, it is available in an ever-increasing range of colours including purple, pink, gold, silver, brown and black.

Uses

- It is ideal for making structures on which to glue flowers or for simply adding a modern interest to your designs.

Bullion wire

Fine, crinkly wire available in a wide range of colours.

Uses

- Threading, binding, scrunching – anything to give decorative detail.

Coloured reel wire

Smooth, thin wire on a reel.

Uses

- Threading, binding, scrunching – anything to give decorative detail.

Methods of wiring

1. Mount wiring

This is a widely used technique for anchoring plant material into a base, or to create a false stem to bind into wedding designs such as bouquets and corsages. There are two types of mount wiring:

a) **Single leg mount –** this will support lighter stems because it creates only one wire 'leg'. It reduces the overall weight of designs in which materials are taped or bound close to the stem end and they therefore do not need extra support – as with a circlet headdress.

Single leg mount

Method

Place the wire underneath the stem near the end, horizontally. Position the wire so that there is a short end and long end either side of the stem. (see sketch) Holding the wire in place with your thumb and forefinger, use your other hand to bend the wire ends down parallel to the stem into a hairpin shape, which will create one long leg.

b) **Double leg mount –** this method has two legs, so will support heavier stems. It is suitable for the long, heavy trailing material in a wired bridal bouquet.

Method

Follow the same method as for the single leg mount, but ensure that the wire is almost equal in length either side of the stem. This will create two legs.

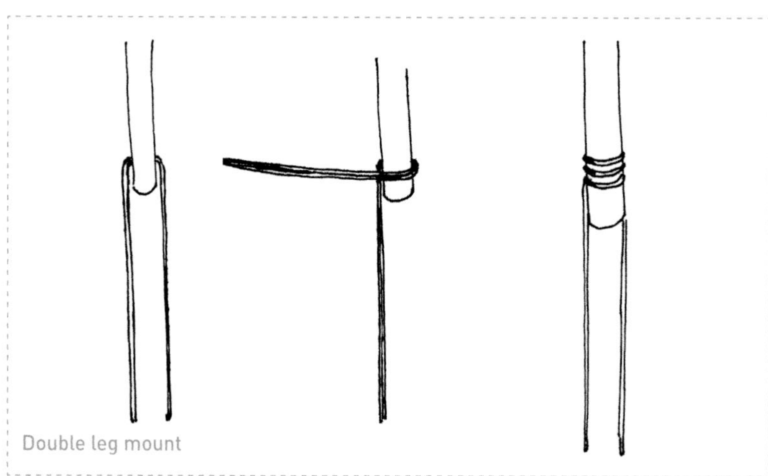

Double leg mount

2. Support wiring

Support wiring strengthens a stem and is used mainly in wedding designs and some funeral work. There are several methods of support wiring for flowers:

a) **Internal –** this is the most discreet method of supporting a stem. It is suitable for hollow or soft fleshy stems, into which the wire can be inserted all the way up to the flower head, as with *Narcissus* or *Anemone*. However, a partial internal wire is often useful if only to give the stem end a little more substance when mount wiring - such as that of a calla lily (*Zantedeschia*).

Method

Insert a long, strong gauge wire up the hollow stem until it bites the inside of the calyx (seed box).

b) **External –** this is the least discreet method because the wire is visible along the length of the stem. *Gerbera* are often support wired in this way after conditioning to help prevent them from curving.

Method

Insert the wire into the base of the flower head (taking care to ensure that it does not protrude through the top). Gently mould and twist the wire down and around the stem. There should be fewer wraps rather than too many close together, which would make the flower feel heavy and look very unnatural. This method can also be used for carnations, which are prone to snapping at the head: gently insert the wire into their calyx before winding around the stem.

c) **Semi-internal –** this is a combination of both internal and external wiring and can be done on fleshy stems. The top half of the stem can be wired internally and the lower part externally.

Method

Insert the wire into the stem approximately 10 cm (4 in) below the flower head. Bend the remaining length of wire around the outside of the stem. If the wire is shorter than the stem, simply insert another stub wire at the point where the first one finished (about 3 cm into the stem) and continue to wrap the remaining wire around the stem.

3. Wired Units

Creating wired units of flowers and foliage is a good way of increasing the length of materials for a design such as a bridal bouquet. In some cases, one unit can make up an entire design such as in a circlet headdress. There are three types of units:

a) **Branching unit –** this is the use of one type of material placed onto one long wire. The advantage of making branching units is that they cut down on bulk and overall weight – both visual and actual. Materials in a branching unit usually graduate in size with smaller heads (or buds) being placed towards the end of the unit and larger heads positioned towards the base and nearer to the centre of a design.

Method

Select a range of different sized flower heads or leaves and grade for size. First, wire each individually using a single or double leg mount. Then tape each one. To cut down on unnecessary bulk, the width of the stem tape should be halved by cutting it along its length. It is surprising how much neater taping of the finer wires becomes as a result.

Take a medium gauge wire such as 0.56 mm and tape the smallest flower or leaf first onto the end of the wire. Once secure, trim any excess length of wire from the flower or leaf as you go, to cut down the weight. Take another flower or leaf and tape it underneath the first one, but leave a small amount of wired stem to give some flexibility. Again, trim any excess wire and repeat this process until the last and largest flower or leaf has been taped onto the wire.

Internal

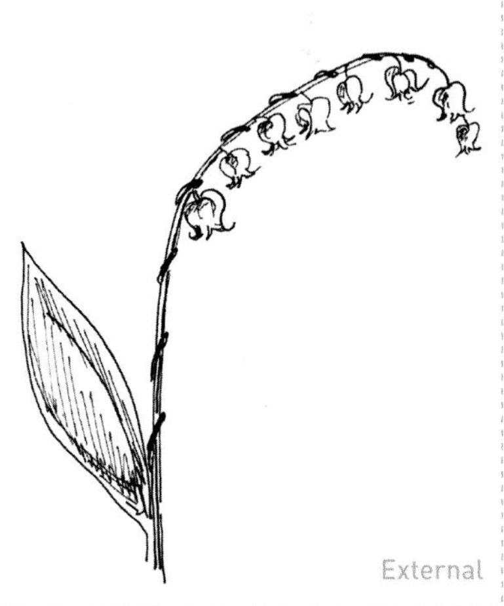
External

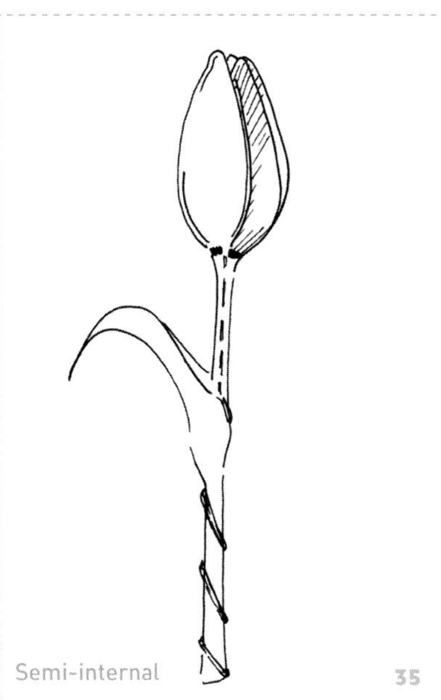
Semi-internal

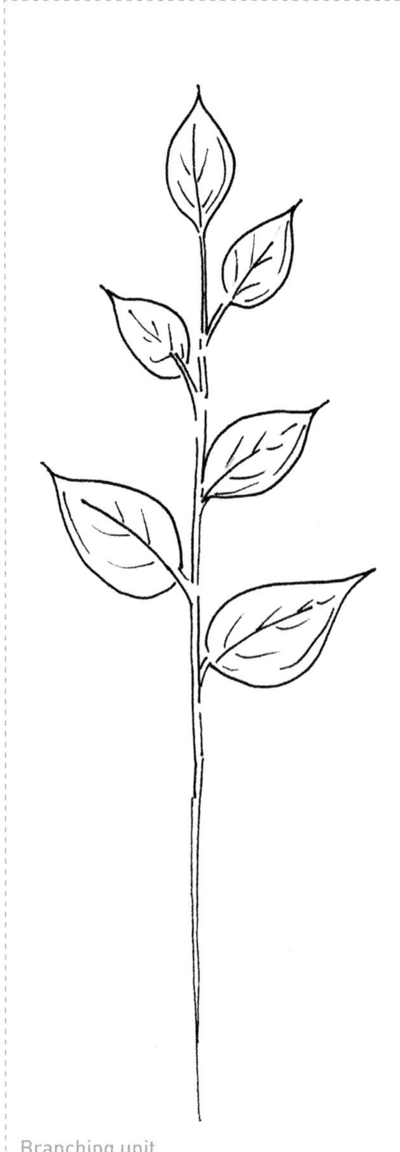

Branching unit

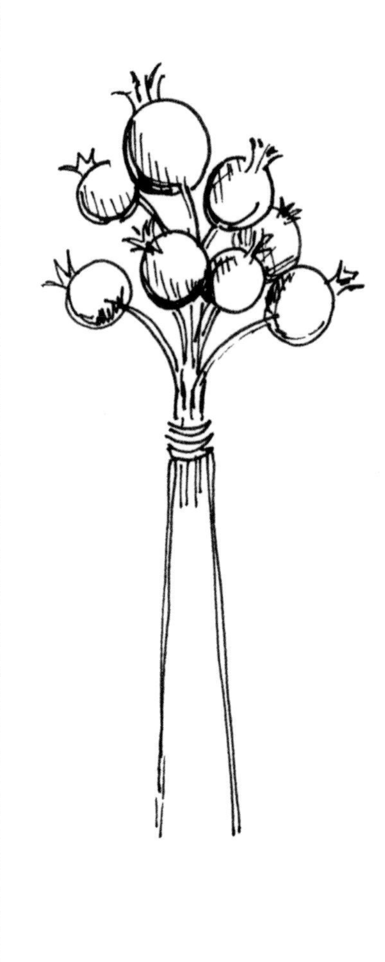

Natural unit

Ribbed unit

b) **Natural unit –** this is simply a small group of stems of one type of material wired together using single or double leg mounts - depending on the weight of the material. Ideal materials for creating a natural unit are *Gypsophila*, waxflower (*Chamelaucium*) and foliage such as *Euonymus*, *Hebe* and sprigs of ming fern (*Asparagus umbellatus*).

c) **Ribbed unit –** this unit is used to make a circlet headdress and consists of a mixture of flowers and foliage, which are taped individually onto one wire to form a mixed unit. Ribbed units can consist of one type of material, but are typified by the use of mixed materials being placed close together to form one solid unit.

Method

Wire all materials individually, then tape each using half-width stem tape. You may include small bunches of materials known as 'natural units', as mentioned above. Once you have prepared all the materials, tape them onto a stronger stub wire – preferably a 0.71 mm, because there should still be flexibility. Keep in mind that all of these materials will add to the weight. A pattern should be adhered to when using mixed materials to ensure even distribution.

Wiring techniques for most commonly used flowers and leaves

There are several different ways to wire flowers. As long as the wire gauge is used correctly and the method chosen is discreet and secure, then it does not matter which method is used. The following techniques vary in terms of 'fiddle factor', but as with all techniques, you will improve with practice.

Individual florets

(*Hyacinthus, Stephanotis, Nerine, Ornithagalum arabicum, Agapanthus*)

These tiny florets are perfect for use in wired headdresses, or other small wired designs such as corsages. This method can be used with a variety of florets taken from larger flowers.

Method

1. Take a light 0.28 mm gauge silver stub wire and bend it into a hairpin. Cross the ends of the wire over until the circular 'head' at the top of the hairpin is small, then twist to secure.

2. Insert the two ends of the wire together into the centre of the head of the floret and gently pull the wires down parallel with the stem. Finally, tape the wires and the stem together. This method is best with delicate florets, because the wires remain straight. Wrapping wires around a soft stem can cause damage.

Roses (*Rosa*)

If the rose is being used short for a buttonhole or corsage, the following method is ideal. If the design is larger - such as a wired bouquet - the stem length should be adjusted accordingly.

Method

1. You could pin the sepals of the rose using a fine 0.28 or 0.32 mm gauge silver stub wire cut into short hairpins. However, doing so often keeps the rose tight and is only really necessary in hot weather when roses are prone to opening very quickly.

2. Place an internal support wire through the short stem, approximately 3 cm (1¼ in) long, using either a 0.71 mm gauge, or 0.90 mm - depending on the size of the rose. Take this as far as the seedbox. Be careful not to pierce the petals as they will bruise and turn brown. Take a similar gauge wire (again, depending on the weight of the rose, but often a 0.90 mm is needed) and double leg mount the stem.

Individual florets

Roses

Carnation (*Dianthus*)

The wiring of a standard carnation differs to that of a rose because carnation petals are less prone to bruising.

Method

1. Take a 0.71 mm or 0.90 mm gauge wire and push it up through the centre of a short stem, approximately 3 cm (1¼ in) long, and right up through the top of the flower.

2. Bend the wire into a small hook and gently pull back down into the flower until the hooked wire will not go any further.

3. Tape the end of the stem and the wire with full-width stem tape.

Lily-of-the-Valley (*Convallaria*)

This method could also be used to support ivy (*Hedera*) trails or *Freesia*.

Method

1. Use fine 0.20 mm gauge green or silver reel wire. Start at the top of the stem making a small hook over the top floret, then very gently wind the wire between the florets.

2. Wind the wire twice around the base of the stem to secure.

3. If extra length or support is needed, double leg mount the stem end using a 0.28 mm, or 0.32 mm gauge stub wire. Then tape using half-width stem tape.

Orchid

Three main types of orchid are used in floristry:

a) ***Phalaenopsis***

Method

1. Insert a fine 0.26 mm stub wire horizontally through the base of the orchid (just above the stem) and bring the legs of the wire down parallel with the orchid stem.

2. Wrap one leg of the wire around the stem and the other leg three times.

b) ***Cymbidium***

Method

1. Insert either a 0.56 mm or 0.71 mm gauge wire (depending on the size and weight of the orchid) internally up the short stem.

2. Take a silver 0.32 mm wire horizontally through the base of the stem finishing as close to the base of the flower as possible.

c) ***Dendrobium***

Method

1. For single heads, insert a fine silver wire (0.20 mm or 0.28 mm gauge) horizontally through the base of the

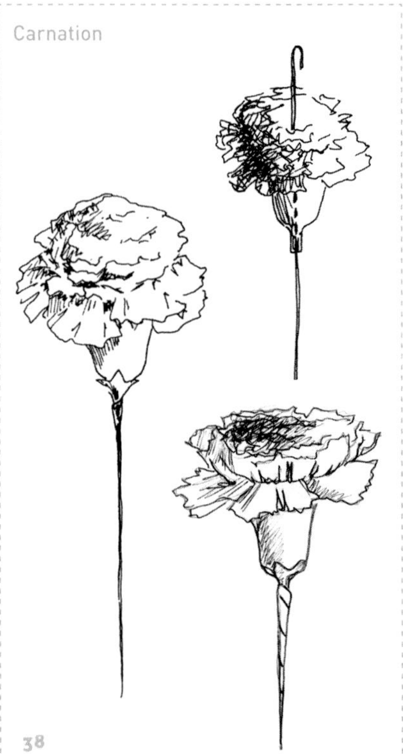

Carnation

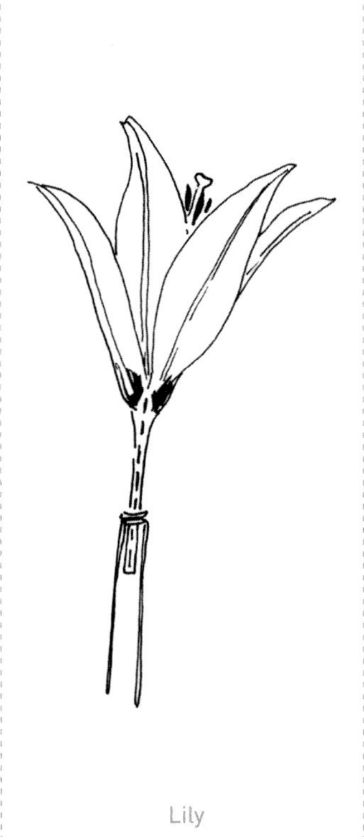

Lily

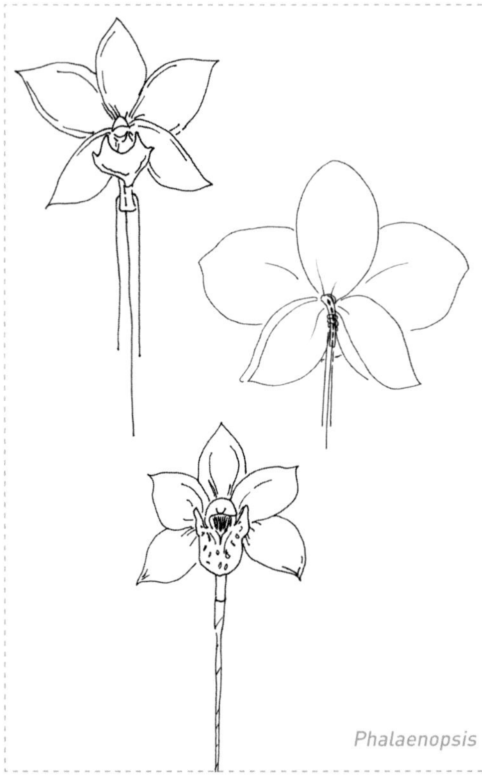

Phalaenopsis

head and bring each end of the wire down gently alongside the stem.

2. Take the nearside wire and wrap around the stem and the other wire to secure.

Lily (*Lilium*)

There are two ways of wiring a lily depending on the length of the stem required. Amaryllis (*Hippeastrum*) heads can also be wired in this way.

Method

1. To include in a bridal bouquet, cut the head off the main stem leaving approx 5 cm (2 in) of stem.

2. Internally wire the stem by inserting a 0.71 mm or 0.90 mm wire (depending on the weight of the lily) up through it as far as the base of the flower – do not allow the wire to protrude through the flower itself.

3. Mount the end of the short stem with a 0.71 mm gauge wire.

Alternatively, if a much shorter head is needed, the stem can be cut as low as possible and the head then 'cross wired'. This means that two heavy silver 0.46 mm, or even 0.56 mm gauge wires can be inserted horizontally through the base of the stem in an X formation. These are then gently bent down in line with the stem and taped. This minimises damage to the head by preventing the need to wrap one of the wires, as with a mount wire. Amaryllis (*Hippeastrum*) heads can also be wired in this way.

Freesia

Freesia florets are very soft and easily damaged, so it is best to wire them intact on a short amount of stem. If individual open flowers are needed, use the method for 'Individual Florets' on page 37.

Method

1. Using a fine silver reel wire (0.28 mm gauge), form a small hook to place around the top bud.

2. Gently bring the wire down and around the other florets and continue down to the end of the stem.

3. The stem end should then be single leg mount wired using a 0.56 mm gauge.

Gerbera

These are usually externally wired around the whole length of the outer stem (see page 40).

Method

1. Using a long, green 0.71 mm wire,

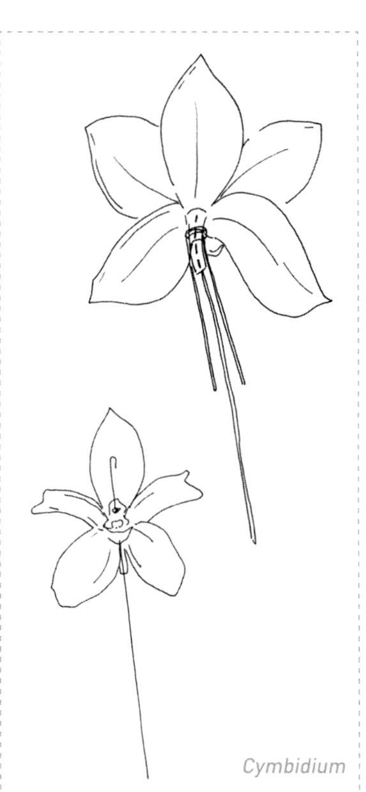

Cymbidium

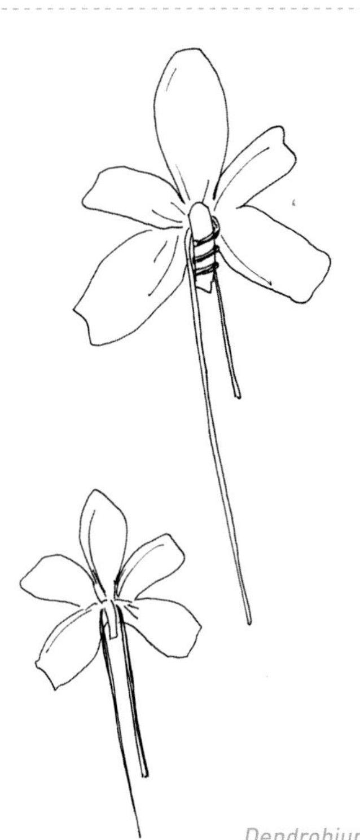

Dendrobium

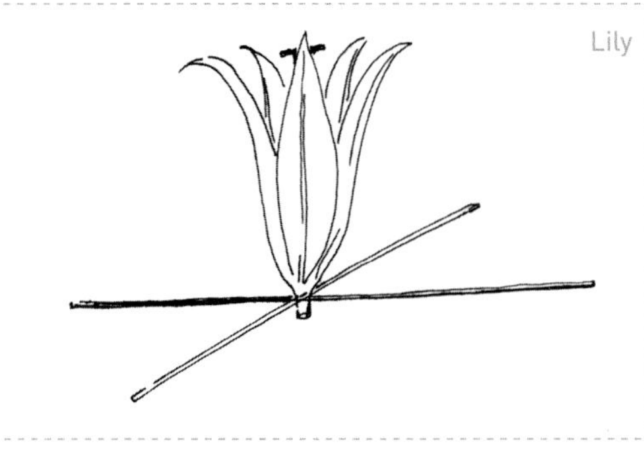

Lily

Freesia

Gerbera

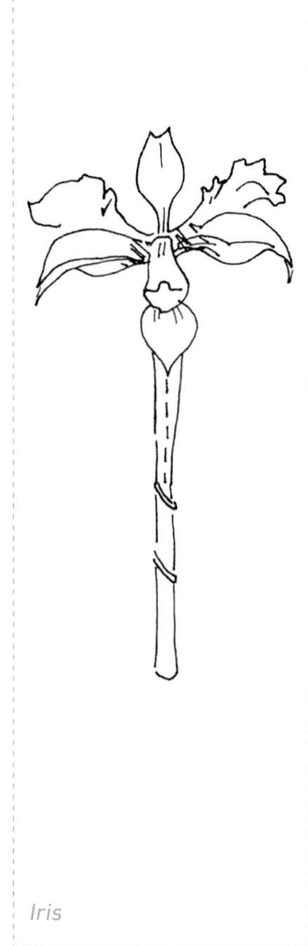
Iris

Amaryllis

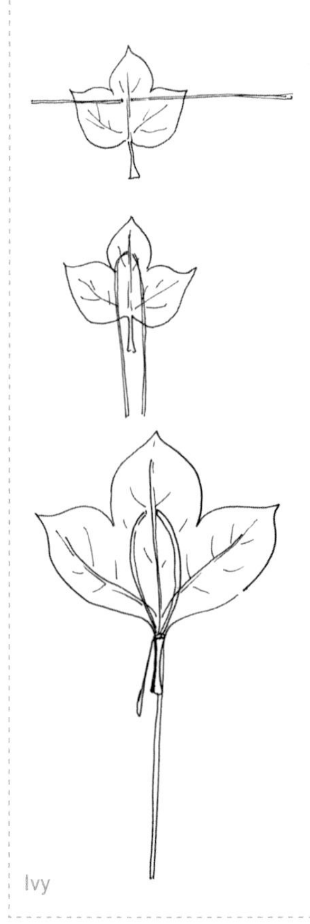
Ivy

gently insert a short length of the wire up into the head ensuring it does not protrude.

2. Take the wire gently down bending it at intervals around the stem. Take care not to wrap the wire too regularly around the stem to prevent it looking 'over wired'.

Tulip (*Tulipa*)

The natural beauty of a tulip as it continues to grow, even as a cut flower, should not be interfered with. They look their best *en masse* in a goldfish bowl being allowed to twist and tumble. However, if they are being used alongside other flowers in mixed designs they do need some support.

Method

1. Wire semi-internally by inserting a green 0.71 mm gauge wire into the stem approximately 5 cm (2 in) below the head.

2. Gently insert the wire up into the stem as far as the head, then take the other end of the wire and gently wind it around the rest of the stem as far as it will go.

Iris can be wired in the same way.

Amaryllis (*Hippeastrum*)

These long, hollow stems really do need support to hold their heavy heads upright. Insert a narrow cane up the centre of the hollow stem.

Ivy (*Hedera*)

Ivy leaves are perfect for inclusion in small, wired designs such as buttonholes and corsages. The most common method of wiring for single leaves is called 'stitching'.

Method

1. Hold the leaf between finger and thumb with the underside of the leaf facing upwards.

2. Take a fine stub wire (0.28 mm or 0.32 mm - depending on the thickness and weight of the leaf) and make a small stitch two thirds of the way up the leaf either side of the central vein.

3. Gently bring the wires down parallel to the stem, and wrap one

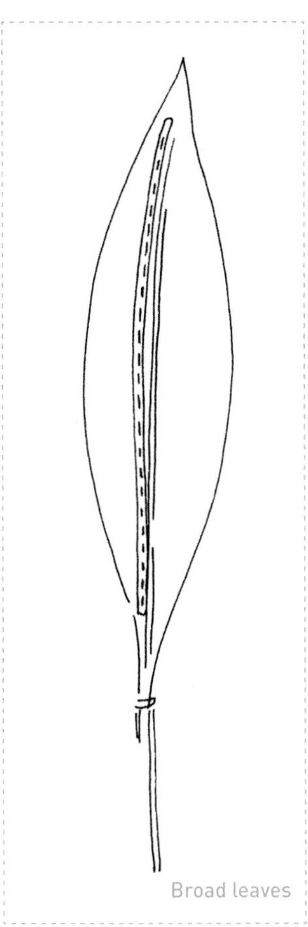
Broad leaves

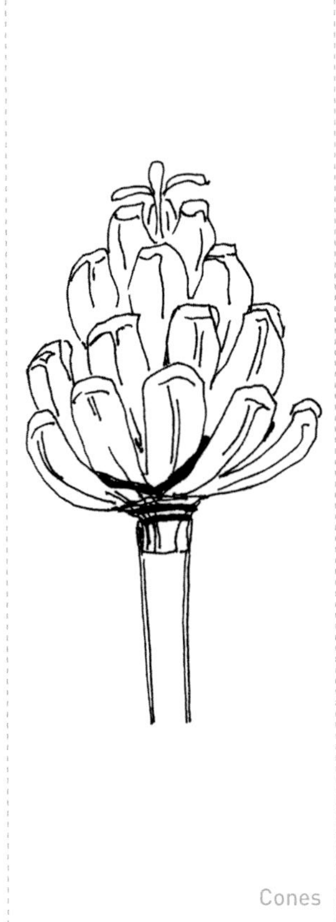
Cones

Fruit

Nuts

around the stem and the other wire. Tape with half-width stem tape.

Broad leaves

(such as *Aspidistra*)

Where broader leaves are being used such as *Aspidistra*, place a long 0.71 mm gauge stub wire along the main vein and tape the wire onto the back of the leaf. (Make sure that the leaf is dry or the tape will not adhere.)

Fruit

Fruit is often a popular choice to include in arrangements, garlands and door wreaths. The following method is for apples, pears, oranges and crab apples.

Method

1. Take a long 0.90 mm gauge stub wire and insert it horizontally through the lower part of the fruit.

2. Bring the two ends of the wire together under the fruit until they meet and twist them together to form a prong.

Cones

A long 0.71 mm stub wire is usually the most suitable. Take the wire around the lower bracts of the cone until it meets. Twist the two ends together to form a 'wire fork', which can be inserted into moss or foam.

Where materials are being inserted into moss and need to defy the pull of gravity (as in a door wreath), ensure that one of the wires is much longer; this will allow it to be pulled through the foundation and then threaded back through to give extra support.

Nuts

These can be trickier to wire as most do not have stems and are hard to pierce.

Method

1. Bend the end of a stub wire (for example a 0.71 mm gauge) to form a small loop.

2. Carefully place a small amount of hot glue on to this and press to the nut. It can be helpful to place the nuts into something (such as an egg carton) to hold them still.

Dad's
Buttonhole
David

chapter 4

Wired designs

This facet of floral design remains as important now as it did prior to the 1950s when foam did not exist and the only handtied was a funeral sheaf.

There are many reasons for this. Primarily, that wiring produces some of the most exquisitely crafted designs that cannot be achieved by any other method. Additionally, the range of decorative wire and accessories now available - including beads, feathers and ribbons - has opened up a whole new world of design possibilities.

Wiring separates the amateur arranger from the professional florist. Classic, formal wired bouquets and bridesmaids' posies, for instance, require much skill and patience. Wired work is incredibly labour intensive and technically involved – far more so than working in foam or creating handtieds, which is why it is much more expensive.

Remember that any design being worn needs to withstand movement, so security is vital.

All wired work should be as neat as possible. The trend for featuring decorative wire has brought with it a temptation to be less neat, but functional wiring should be as lightweight (yet secure) and unobtrusive as possible. However, the results are worth the extra effort.

There are essentially two types of wired work – functional and decorative. For those new to floristry, it is wise initially to focus on learning and perfecting the functional wiring techniques and essential support methods as discussed in Chapter 3. The decorative work will naturally follow later once you have gained the knowledge and expertise of functional methods.

The buttonhole

Use

By incorporating slightly different materials, a design classic is given a new look.

The buttonhole is in essence a single flower worn by a man for decorative adornment on his lapel. These days it tends to be reserved for special occasions (notably weddings), but during the Victorian and Edwardian eras it was a gentleman's fashion accessory.

The range of flower materials used could be anything from a sprig of lily-of-the-valley (*Convallaria*), to *Gardenia*, or *Camellia* blooms. This was usually backed by a leaf or a small spray of foliage - just as buttonholes are today.

To keep these delicate blooms lasting all day, small filigree silver holders were used which contained a small glass phial to hold water. These were typically worn behind the lapel, though it is possible to buy modern versions (with a magnet attached) to be worn as a decorative feature in the front of the lapel.

From the 1950s, the carnation (*Dianthus*) became very popular for buttonholes – in fact, bridal bouquets were often made entirely of carnations with *Asparagus setaceus* fern as an accompaniment.

Today, roses are a popular choice for bridal buttonholes. They are often made more distinctive with the inclusion of decorative foliage and grasses, or items such as wire, beads and feathers.

Calla lilies (*Zantedeschia*) are also used; avoid the large ones because they can be difficult to keep upright on a lapel and they can look visually unbalanced.

Cymbidium orchids are an excellent choice for buttonholes; they last well out of water and come in several colours. Their star-like form often looks more distinctive than other flower shapes and they are still considered a choice flower.

The rounder, flatter *Phalaenopsis* and *Vanda* orchids are also lovely. The *Phalaenopsis* is a little more delicate, though, and the *Vanda* is much more leathery in texture. Both are available with small or larger heads. For a larger head, it is better to buy *Phalaenopsis* as a cut flower rather than as a pot plant.

Flowers and foliage

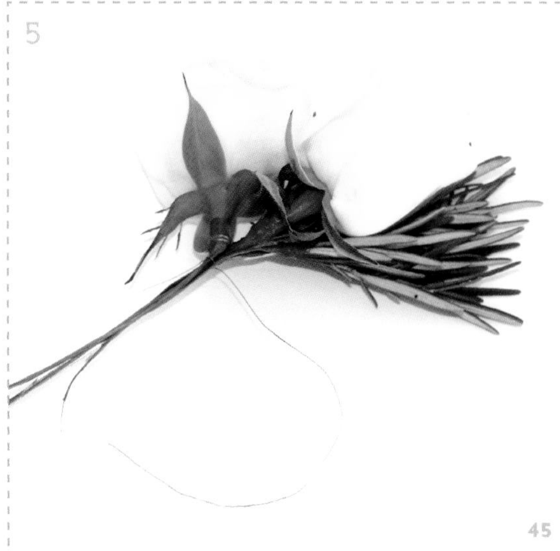

Materials

Flowers and foliage	Sundries
1 stem white *Rosa* 'Avalanche'	green stem tape
1 sprig small-leaved *Hebe*	0.32, 0.40 and 0.90 mm
3 x stems white *Astilbe*	gauge stub wires
2 x *Galax* leaves	
1 sprig rosemary (*Rosmarinus*)	

Tips

- Buttonholes can be themed for special functions. For example, a country design could feature wheat (*Triticum*) as an accompaniment.
- Select only those materials that you know will tolerate being out of water for several hours. Avoid all spring flowers and other notable soft herbaceous materials.

Method

1. Ensure you have conditioned all material well before use - particularly the roses (see page 192).

2. Cut the foliage to the required short length and defoliate the stems. Then, single leg mount each with a stub wire (see page 34) - the wire's thickness is always dependent upon the weight. Bind the wired foliage with stem tape (cut the tape in half to reduce its width).

3. Single leg mount each of the three stems of *Astilbe*.

4. Select the best rose bloom and if necessary remove two or three of the outer petals, which often look unsightly. Cut the stem just below the seedbox leaving a small amount. If the rose is large and heavy, you will need a 0.90 mm gauge wire. Insert this up into the centre of the stem as far as the seedbox. Never allow the wire to come too far up into the rose head itself or it will bruise and discolour the petals. If the rose has a smaller head and is lighter in weight, then a 0.71 mm gauge will suffice.

5. Cover the stem and wire with (full-width) stem tape, concentrating on the point where the wire meets the stem. Avoid covering too much of the natural stem with the tape. It is not necessary to cover the full length of the wire since all stems will be cut a little shorter.

6. Arrange all materials and bind together using fine silver reel wire.

7. Once you have included all wired materials into the binding point, bring the reel wire down vertically alongside the stems and trim to a short length, usually 3 – 5 cm (1 – 2 in). Cover all stems with tape to form one single stem. Ensure the end of the stem is sealed completely and that no bare wires are visible.

8. Place a pearl-headed (or coloured) pin through the stem for attachment to the lapel.

Alternative materials

The corsage

Use

A corsage is by definition a small design made for adornment - usually to be worn by a woman for a formal occasion. While it is usually attached to a coat lapel or worn below the shoulder, the corsage is in fact so versatile that it can be adapted for use as a wristlet, headdress, hat, or handbag spray.

The corsage differs from the buttonhole in that it contains more than one flower and can be simple or very intricate.

As with all wired designs, care should be taken to select materials that will tolerate being out of water for several hours.

Corsages should be as lightweight as possible and the lightest wires (which will still support) should be used wherever possible.

Materials

Flowers and foliage

2 x *Cymbidium* orchid heads
1 piece of contorted or cork screw hazel (*Corylus avellana* 'Contorta')
2 x *Galax* or ivy (*Hedera*) leaves
1 *Leucadendron*
6 x *Hypericum* berries
2 x pieces bear grass (*Xerophyllum lenax*)

Sundries

green stem tape
8 x silver 0.28 mm gauge wires
2 x 0.71 mm gauge wires
4 x 0.56 mm gauge wires
0.28 mm reel wire (to bind stems)
pearl-headed pin, or another means of attachment such as magnet

Flowers and foliage

5

5

Method

1. Insert an internal wire up into the centre of the orchid stem (cut short) and then add a lighter 0.56 mm gauge wire as an external mount (see page 34).

2. Mount wire clusters of *Leucadendron* leaves. Thread the *Hypericum* berries onto the grass and single leg mount each of the four ends of the grass with fine stub wire.

3. Stitch wire the ivy leaves and mount wire the hazel stems (see page 34).

4. Tape all the wired stems individually (see page 32).

5. Bind together all the stems placing the orchids centrally and using the leaves at the base as a collar. Place the hazel to the back of the orchids and tape all these stems together as a single stem.

6. Attach by using a pin, a T-bar or corsage magnet.

Alternative flowers

The full range of orchids - including Singapore orchid (*Dendrobium*), moth orchid (*Phalaenopsis*), or *Cymbidium* orchid - *Helleborus foetidus*, *Gardenia*, roses and small calla lilies (*Zantedeschia*).

Other suitable smaller flowers are *Stephanotis* and *Freesia* - though the latter can be a challenge to wire for inexperienced hands.

Tip

Before adding a magnet, check that the wearer does not have a pacemaker as the magnet will affect it. And do not place it near a watch as it may stop.

Wrist corsage

Use

Wrist corsages are widely used in the United States of America for proms, dances and parties and at weddings for the mothers of the bride and groom. They are also becoming popular in Europe.

There are a wide range of mechanics that can be used such as ribbon, decorative wire and specialist floral wrist bracelets. Here, we have used a Velcro wristlet manufactured by OASIS® which is not expensive, is easy to use and is very effective; the strap is fully adjustable and very secure. Typically, corsages are small, for comfort. They do not damage clothing and can be easily removed later in the evening.

Materials

Flowers and foliage

3 - 5 *Galax* leaves
2 x *Phalaenopsis* orchid heads

Sundries

1 OASIS® Velcro wristlet or similar
floral adhesive or any strong adhesive
a length of very thin 'string' ribbon
1 length of light gauge wire

Method

1. With floral adhesive, glue the *Galax* leaves onto the wristlet to cover the metal base. Allow to dry.

2. Using the glue sparingly, attach the orchid heads to the *Galax* leaves. Allow to dry; this will take about 15 minutes.

3. If you wish to add ribbon, make a bow with the 'string' ribbon. Create eight 2.5 cm (1 in) loops. Gather in the centre with the fine wire. Trim the wire and glue the bow between the flowers.

Tips

The finished corsage is fragile, so place it in a cellophane bag to retain its moisture, before packing it in a tissue-lined box to protect from damage.

Alternative flowers

Bold, flat flowers such as mini *Gerbera*, *Gardenia*, mini *Cymbidium* and tea roses work well. *Freesia* also look most effective.

Wire-based brooches

Use

Decorative adornments to wear on any occasion.

The vast array of decorative wires now available has resulted in myriad colourful and highly decorative floral accessories. The different shapes of wired brooches shown here, all using the same technique, illustrate just a few examples. The structure can be made in advance and kept permanently – particularly if beads, feathers and silk florets are used.

In terms of attachment, T-bars with safety pins are excellent and much easier and safer for the wearer than traditional pins. Corsage magnets are also secure, but remember it is essential to check that the wearer is not fitted with a pacemaker, because the magnet will affect its function.

Materials

For the brooches' outlines, use aluminium wire in colours to suit.

For the heart
1 reel each of cerise and purple bullion wires
pink smooth decorative wire
about 20 small purple beads

For the triangle
lime green smooth decorative wire
two-tone textured wire

For the circle
1 reel each of black and silver bullion wires
pearl-headed pin
Ornithogalum arabicum pips

Method

1. Fashion a shape of your choice with the aluminium wire.
2. Attach the ends together using a touch of hot glue. Disguise the glue when it is set by wrapping with bullion wire.
3. For the dense effect in the heart and circle shapes, unravel the bullion wires simultaneously until there is sufficient to fill the shape – this will require about 3 m (10 ft). Scrunch these together and mould into the desired shape.
4. Stitch this inside the aluminium wire outline – usually the smooth, slightly heavier, coloured wires are better suited than finer, wavy bullion wire.
5. To form the green triangular brooch, wrap a combination of the textured and smooth lime green wires randomly around and within the triangular shape until it is filled. To make a more masculine adornment for a lapel, finish now.
6. To make the heart, wire or glue beads onto any of the structures – cold gluing is easier. The same can be done with pips of flowers such as the tiny black-eyed *Ornithogalum arabicum* floret used on the black circular brooch.
7. Threaded *Hypericum* berries work well. Thread the smooth decorative wire through the berry; make a line with the required number. These berries are ideal because they do not exude sap or disintegrate like most berries, which is why they are so widely used in floristry.

7

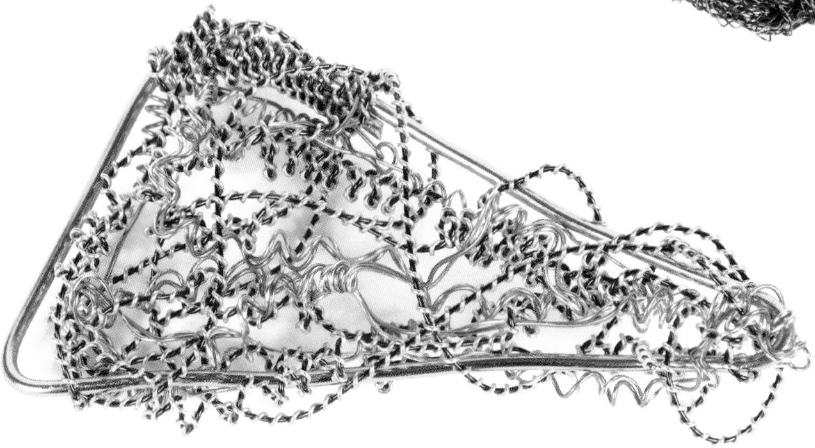

Tips

Do not over-decorate or it will look fussy and hide the beauty of the wired structure – simplicity is key.

Alternative flowers

Materials need to be able to tolerate being out of water without wilting and to be small and lightweight.

These are ideal: a range of florets / pips from larger flowers such as *Agapanthus*, *Stephanotis*, statice (*Limonium*), *Dendrobium* orchids, grasses such as flexi grass (*Ficinea fascicularis*), bear grass (*Xerophyllum tenax*) and China grass (*Liriope muscari*).

Wired posy

Use

This design would suit a bride who wants a light bouquet that is not too bulky to hold. It is more formal-looking and is generally neat in appearance. This effect cannot be achieved either on a foam holder, or by tying.

This simple, compact posy is lightweight to carry and the orchids are tolerant of being out of water for several hours, making them a good choice for a wired design.

Note that as with all wired designs, extra time should be allowed for preparation.

Materials

Flowers and foliage

1 stem (with approximately 10 to 12 heads) *Cymbidium* orchid

5 x stems sweet William (*Dianthus barbatus*)

2 x stems coral fern (*Gleichenia polypodioides*)

5 x *Galax* or ivy leaves

Sundries

selection of stub wires: 0.32 mm, 0.45 mm and 0.71 mm gauge

stem tape – green or brown depending on the colour of the flowers chosen

narrow satin ribbon (for the handle)

fine 0.28mm gauge binding wire

Flowers and foliage

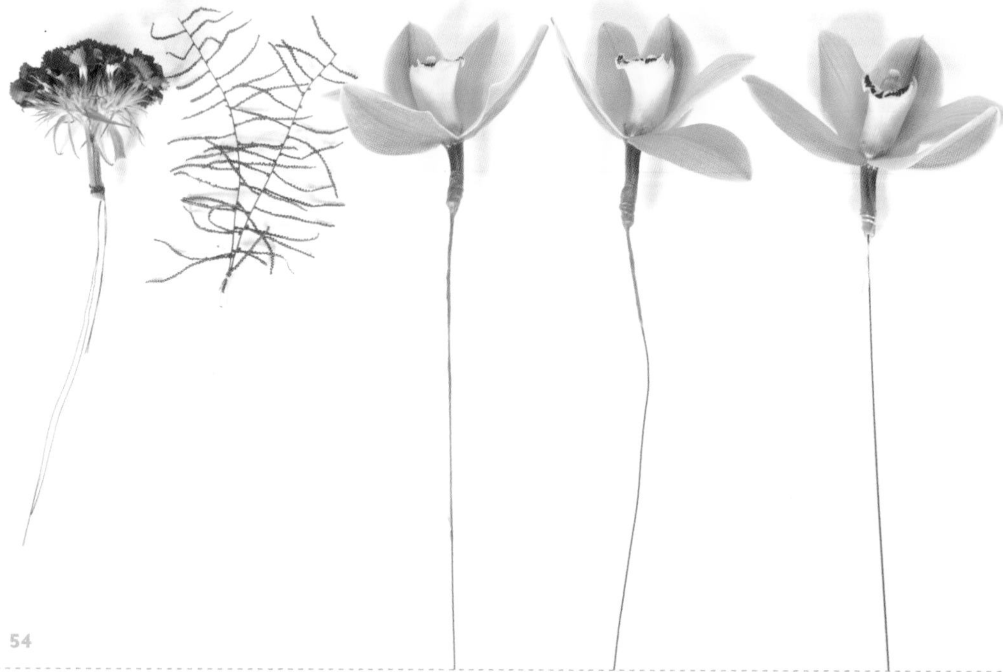

Method

1. Cut the orchid stems to approximately 5 cm (2 in). Wire the heads individually (see page 38).

2. Cut the sweet William stems to about 2.5 cm (1 in). Double leg mount each using 0.56 mm gauge wire.

3. Stitch-wire the five *Galax* leaves (see page 40). Make a small satin bow with the ribbon.

4. Cut the coral fern into approximately six smaller pieces and double leg mount using 0.32 mm silver wire, as this is very delicate.

5. Once you have wired all the materials, tape them. Always use half-width tape for lighter wires and the full-width for heavier wires.

6. Once you have taped all the materials individually, attach a stay wire (see page 38) to the orchids, sweet William and coral fern. Some of the other materials may also need extra length so they can be bound into the binding point.

7. Start with the central orchid and place one of the sweet Williams directly next to it. Attach the end of the fine binding wire to the stem.

8. Bind in two more orchid heads as close as possible, then another two sweet Williams.

9. After every second or third flower you add, wrap the binding wire firmly around. The binding point should remain in one position as far as possible. Remember to add in the coral fern as you continue.

10. Once you have included all materials, add the *Galax* leaves as close as possible to the base in order to hide the mechanics.

11. Trim the binding wire and the wires that now form the handle. The length should be just wider than the width of your hand. Seal with full-width stem tape. Wrap with satin ribbon. In this example, a deep red colour would be effective to pick out the colour in the centre of the orchid and also the sweet William. Add a bow if you wish.

Tips

Use longer 260 mm length stub wires to achieve length for the outer flowers.

Try to include unusual materials such as herbs and other garden foliage or grasses to add interest to commercially grown flowers.

Alternative materials

Flowers

The *Cymbidium* orchids lend themselves to this wired posy, as their stems are too short to use in a handtied. Roses could be used, but they would usually be tied not wired. Small *Anthurium*, amaryllis (*Hippeastrum*) heads.

Foliage

Flexi grass (*Ficinea fascicularis*) used in loops, umbrella fern (*Sticherus umbellatus*).

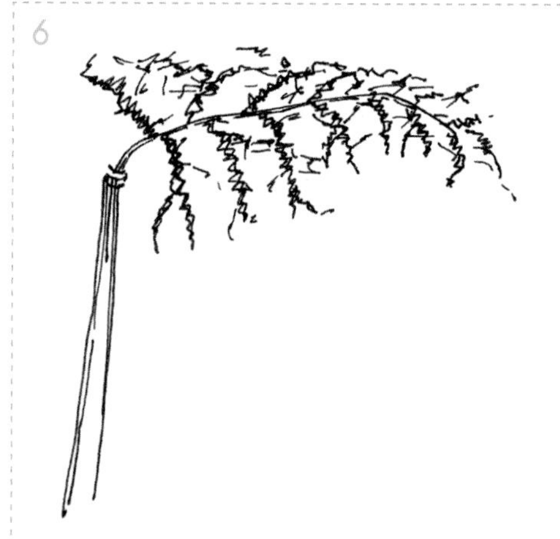

6

7

8

Wired handbag

Use

This intricate little bag can be used for a number of occasions - as a wedding accessory for a bridesmaid, perhaps, or at other functions such as a May Ball or a special evening event.

The beauty of this design, which uses decorative wire and artificial flowers, is that you can use it again long after any fresh flowers have faded. The pink and green wire combination used here would be ideal for someone wearing a cerise pink or green dress.

Materials

Sundries

2 x reels decorative reel wire
1 reel bullion wire
square from a piece of cardboard
1 artificial orchid
fine deep pink satin ribbon
beads

Method

1. Cut a square from a piece of cardboard to the shape and size you want the bag to be. Note that the bag will be slightly larger than the card.

2. Gather the ends of all three wires together, but keep them on their reels.

3. Begin by wrapping the wires around a pen four times to create coils. Then leave a short gap of about 5 cm (2 in) before doing four more coils. Continue with this pattern until you have used approximately three quarters of each of the reel wires. Note: the bullion wire will run out first, because it is smaller so just re-join with the second reel.

4. Once you have created enough coiled wire to be wrapped around the card several times, secure the wire ends to any part of the card using a piece of adhesive wire. Continue to wrap the wires around the card, working up and down to cover all of the surface area. Continue back up to the top of the card. At this point, take the wire above the card to form the handle. Reinforce this handle to the rest of the bag with about three more sections of the wire. Wrapping the wire down the card and back up each time as it evolves.

5. Once you have reached the end of the coiled wire, secure the ends to the nearest section of the wire bag. Push any protruding ends back into the structure.

6. Using the lighter bullion wire, thread a long length of the pink or green beads ensuring there is a 10 cm (4 in) space between each - otherwise they will look packed together and too uniform. Twist the two wires together under each bead to secure in place.

7. These threaded beads can then be wrapped around the bag. It is also possible to include them before you finish the bag itself, so that they sit closer to the bag rather than on top. However do not include the beads too early into the structure or the wire will disguise them.

8. Stitch the sides of the design with smooth reel wire in the same colour wire as used for the bag. This is important or the bag will not stay attached when it is held by the handle.

9. If desired, you can also use decorative ribbon by simply wrapping it around the bag – though you do need to do this – alongside the last few wraps of the coiled wire so that it is properly incorporated. The illustrated design contains some thin pink ribbon, which is interlaced with the last three coils of wire.

10. At this point, extract the piece of card from inside the bag. Holding the bag firmly, use a pair of pliers to grip and pull the card out of the design.

11. Finish the bag with an orchid. This can be either mount wired (see page 34) or glued on. When using silk flowers, hot glue is fine.

Tips

Allow plenty of floor space when fashioning the wire coils. You need enough room for the wires to snake along the floor in lines so that they do not tangle.

chapter 5

Handtied designs

Handtieds have become, arguably, the most popular commercial design in floristry. Their adaptability allows them to be used for a variety of occasions - including presentation gifts, funeral tributes and bridal bouquets.

European floral design has influenced and encouraged a vast range of embellishments that can be added to handtieds - such as twig structures and collars. Leaf manipulation can be used in minimalistic contemporary styles to show off a distinctive form to its best advantage.

The flower materials used will dictate the theme or style of a handtied. For instance, the use of tropical flowers gives a vibrant, exotic look, while open roses mixed with soft herbaceous flowers lend themselves to a romantic, summery feel.

Tied work for weddings and funerals should always be left unwrapped (except for protection in transit). Packaging can be distracting and the beauty of the materials should be maximised as much as possible on these occasions.

Bridal handtieds should have their stems wrapped with a matching ribbon to protect the dress. The stems are usually cut a little shorter than those in conventional handtieds. To achieve a flowing feel to the bouquet, emphasis should be placed on trailing delicate materials such as long *Asparagus* trails, *Amaranthus* and beautifully arching *Euphorbia fulgens*.

In recent times, wedding magazines have popularised the tighter Biedermeier-style of handtied for brides' bouquets. These are often made entirely of roses locked head to head to create a perfectly round posy shape. They are sometimes finished with a simple collar of leaves, twigs or even feathers as a contrast.

This chapter shows examples from the range of different styles of handtieds with illustrated step-by-step explanations on how to construct each one from scratch.

Throughout we have used appropriate seasonal flowers alongside some year-round staples to give the designs more interest.

Basic handtied bouquet

Use

A mixed handtied is a classic design that is given for birthdays, thank-you gifts, get-well wishes, or simply for a vase to save the recipients arranging it themselves.

The key feature of its construction is the spiralling stem technique in which all stems are placed successively at a 45° angle in the same direction. Once this is mastered, any handtied can be easily achieved. They work equally well with either one type of flower (such as roses, or anemones), or a mixture of flowers. Mixing flowers often evokes a specific look such as the country theme using *Tanacetum*, *Matricaria*, spray roses and *Pannicum* grasses.

Materials

Flowers and foliage

7 x pink roses
7 x spray *Chrysanthemum*
5 x *Allium*
5 x lisianthus (*Eustoma*)
5 x pink *Paeonia*
2/3 bunch *Eucalyptus cinerea*
3 x *Alstroemeria*

Sundries

twine, bind wire or polypropylene
raffia or ribbon
Fabtex® or Cellophane
tissue paper
stapler
extra square of Cellophane for aqua pack

Tips

- Keep any curving flowers to the outer edges of the handtied as they will look better here than towards the centre.
- Check the design before tying it off. Any flowers that need to be moved can be gently taken out at this stage and re-inserted where necessary - but only if they have a strong stem. If you wish to place a special or large bloom in the centre of a compact handtied, this is your opportunity.
- Ensure the wrapping material is not too large for the design, or it will swamp the flowers.

Alternative materials

Flowers

mini *Gerbera*, sunflowers (*Helianthus*).

Foliage and berries

Salal tips (*Gaultheria shallon*), *Hypericum*.

3

5

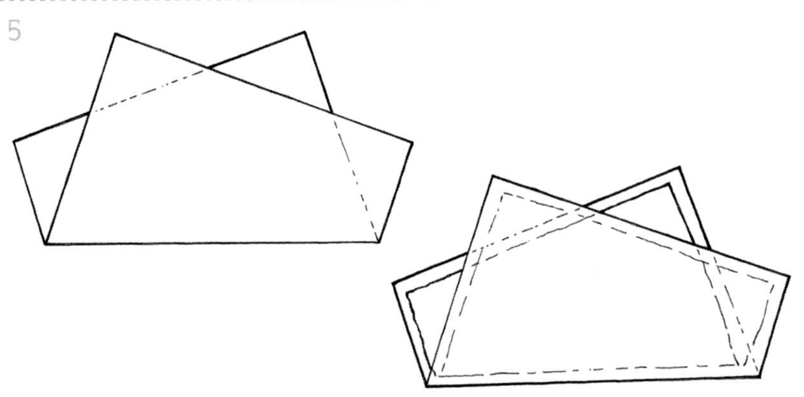

Method

1. Defoliate each stem to approximately two thirds of the way up. This must be done at this stage. Clean stems are an important feature of this design.

2. Take one stem of either flower or foliage and hold it upright. Take another stem and place on a 45° angle with the tip / head of the flower / foliage going over the back of the hand.

3. Place successive flowers and foliage in exactly this way and do not change direction. You can use your other hand to turn the bouquet and alleviate the weight from one hand. This simple method of placing each flower on an angle in exactly the same position will give you spiralled stems.

4. Once you have placed all the materials into a spiral, use twine, bind wire (paper-covered wire), or polypropylene ribbon to tie the stems firmly. Ensure they are not loose or the design will fall apart.

5. Cut a square of wrapping fabric or tissue and fold diagonally offset so that there are two peaks at the top. If the handtied is small, one square should wrap around completely but medium or larger bouquets will need two squares. Different colours may be used. If you are using tissue paper and Cellophane, the tissue needs to be placed on top of the Cellophane prior to folding so that it will not come into contact with water.

6. Wrap the folded square/s around the tied design and tie again at the base. The top sides of the wrapping will need to be secured with either adhesive tape or staples.

7. If the design is to be out of water for longer than 10 minutes, use an aqua pack. To make one, cut a generous square of Cellophane (enough to come above the binding point with a little to spare). Tie securely, then add a pre-made bow fashioned from a decorative material such as raffia or ribbon.

8. To make the bow, see Techniques page 191.

9. Once you have attached the bow, add water to your aqua pack. Hold the bouquet upright and carefully pour water into the centre - it will flow into the aqua pack.

6

7

9

Compact spring handtied with ivy detail

Use

This handtied would look equally at home in a vase or - with some appropriate adaptations - carried by a bride.

Generally, bridal bouquets need to be smaller and more compact than most gift handtieds. Meticulous attention must be given to their safety for carrying; there should be no sharp wires or pins protruding to snag the dress. Florists finish the handle (on the morning just prior to delivery) by first binding it with stem tape, and then concealing this with satin ribbon. It is secured with pearl-headed or diamanté pins.

Do remember that it is easy to underestimate how many flowers will be needed for even a modest size compact handtied. When using flower material in such a tightly packed fashion, you will need many more stems than if there is space within the design.

Materials

Flowers and foliage

20 x pink *Anemone*
30 x purple *Anemone*
10 x ivy (*Hedera*) trails

Sundries

paper-covered bind wire (green)
3 x long 0.71mm gauge stub wires
3 x long 0.90 mm gauge stub wires
green stem tape
polypropylene ribbon

Method

1. Prepare the collar by forming a thick circle of several ivy trails curling round each other. Wind the trails over and under each other to give a more relaxed look.
2. Secure with a small amount of green paper-covered bind wire.
3. Choose the neatest side of the ivy collar to be the upper side and attach three pre-taped 0.71 mm gauge wires at equal intervals on the underside. Twist the pieces of each wire together to secure.
4. If the wire is not long or strong enough to form the handle, extend the 0.71 mm wire by placing a slightly heavier 0.90 mm wire against it. Tape them together with stem tape in either green or brown - whichever is the most discreet.
5. Holding the collar in one hand, start by placing the first few *Anemone* stems into the centre of the holder.
6. Follow the basic handtied method described on page 66 to point 3.
7. Once all materials are included in the design, use polypropylene ribbon to tie the stems and the wire handle of the ivy collar together.
8. Cut the stem ends. Proportionally, the distance from the tie point upwards should be two thirds and the distance downwards one third.
9. Add a final ivy trail (or two) to cover the tie point.

Tips

- Ensure the size of the collar is determined by the amount of flowers used. If the hole is too big, you will need more flowers to fill it. However, if it is too narrow, the effect may be hidden once flowers are inserted.
- Use a softer tying material such as polypropylene ribbon to secure soft stems like *Anemone*. Bind wire is only suitable for hard, woodier stems such as roses. Choose an olive green colour, which is less obtrusive.

3

5

Alternative materials

Flowers

Tulips, roses, lily of the valley (*Convallaria*).

Foliage

Stitched glossy *Camellia* leaves would give a more elegant look for the collar.

Hostess-style handtied bouquet

Use

This classic, mixed hostess-style handtied is a popular design that is now used for a variety of occasions including birthdays and thank-you gifts.

This is a summer version, using appropriate seasonal materials. When there is an abundance of seasonal flowers available, it is far nicer to use these than some of the flowers we see throughout the year.

Materials

Flowers and foliage

9 x pink roses
9 x *Astilbe*
7 x *Sedum*
7 x salal (*Gaultheria*) foliage
7 x pink cornflower (*Centaurea*)
7 x *Cestrum*

Sundries

2 x squares sisal fabric

1

1

2

Method

1. Follow the method described for the basic handtied on page 66 to point 4.

2. Cut squares of sisal fabric. Fold over and wrap one folded square around the handtied. Tape in place. Offset the second folded square around the bouquet and tape. Disguise the tape with a ribbon bow.

Tip

Staples look neater than clear tape, which can collect dirt from fingertips.

Spring handtied with a collar

Use

This display of spring flowers can be used as a corporate design (see chapter 8), or in the home.

Compact handtieds often benefit from having a collar, which both complements the design and helps protect any vulnerable flowers on the outside. The weeping birch (*Betula pendula*) in this collar is a natural seasonal complement to spring flowers. Like all deciduous trees, the birch sheds its leaves in winter and does not re-grow until late spring. This makes its fine, bare branches ideal for manipulating into a circular collar.

If you are using tulips, remember that they continue to grow after cutting, so their position and height will alter quite significantly in an arrangement.

Materials

Flowers and foliage
20 - 25 x hyacinths (*Hyacinthus*)
8 - 10 x birch (*Betula pendula*) stems

Sundries
3 x long (260 mm) 0.90 mm gauge wires
brown stem tape
tying materials such as string, paper-covered wire, raffia or polypropylene ribbon (olive green would be the best colour)

Tips

- To avoid using larger quantities of flower materials, ensure that the collar is not too large, particularly on the inside. When flower stems are defoliated they lose much of their volume, so more are needed.
- If you are using a glass container, cover the tie point with something attractive. In this case a little of the birch would link well with the collar.

Alternative flowers

If whites are the preference, the following would be suitable:
All year - germini, roses, lisianthus (*Eustoma*).
Spring - *Iris*, paper whites (*Narcissi*).
Summer - *Hydrangea paniculata, Nerine, Nigella.*

Method

1. First prepare the collar by twisting the birch into a circular shape. Secure it by folding the end under itself. Continue to add further birch stems until the required width of circular collar is achieved.

2. Make the handle of the collar by pushing one of the long 0.90 mm wires (pre-taped with the brown stem tape) through the birch on the underside of the collar. Secure by twisting the wire around on itself, flush to the birch collar.

   Place another two wires, roughly equidistant from each other, to form three legs - you will use these to hold the collar while feeding the flower stems through.

3. Defoliate flower materials until the stems are clean. Be gentle when pulling off leaves because the soft spring stems can snap easily.

4. Hold the collar by the taped wire handle with one hand and begin by placing one flower into the centre of the collar.

5. Follow the method described to make a handtied on page 66 to point 3.

6. Aim for a very gradual domed shape. The flowers in the centre should be a touch higher than those on the outside. The outer flowers should be on the same level as the collar.

7. Finally, tie the stems and the wire handle together and trim fairly short. Place in a suitable container.

1

2

5

Handtied featuring weaving

Use

This is a different way of using a collar to enhance a tied design. In this illustration, the importance of using a well chosen container to achieve the overall look can be seen.

The collar has been made from *Salix* (the classic weeping willow synonymous with river banks) and decorated with the versatile *Craspedia*. There are relatively few flowers which possess a flexible quality to their stems, but *Craspedia* is one that does. Its characteristic drumstick shape works well in a variety of designs and has longevity making it ideal for corperate designs (see chapter 8).

This handtied is comprised of yellow tulips, which have a slightly longer life if placed directly in water. Remember that tulips will grow taller after a few hours in water.

Materials

Flowers and foliage

10 x *Craspedia*
35 x tulips
10 x stems weeping willow (*Salix*)

Sundries

3 x long 0.90 mm gauge stub wires (for handle on collar)
green stem tape (to cover wires)
tying material such as raffia, string, or polypropylene ribbon (an olive green colour is the least obtrusive)

Alternative flowers and foliage

For compact handtieds, round forms often work best to create a perfect circular design. However, there are not many alternatives to *Craspedia* as few flowers have that degree of flexibility. Grasses could be used instead.

The collar needs to be made from a fairly flexible material so twigs must be fresh and still contain sap. Always put them in water once freshly cut to retain flexibility.

For the handtied - *Ranunculus* and roses.
For the collar – birch (*Betula pendula*) and dogwood (*Cornus*).

Method

1. Construct the collar by curving the first stem of willow into a circular form and bending the end of the stem over and under the circle to secure it.

2. Continue this method with the other stems of willow until a suitable size of circular collar has been formed.

3. Secure the three wires to the underside of the frame. Place the wire through the willow then bend the wire and twist to secure. Place the three wires equidistant to form a handle (see page 74).

4. Support the ring on a tall container or hold by the collar. Wind and twist *Craspedia* through the willow ring securing with short lengths of bindwire.

5. Follow the basic handtied method described on page 66 to point 3.

6. Create a shallow, slightly domed effect by placing the central flowers slightly higher and the outer flowers so that they are level with the height of the collar.

Tips

- Always cut the stems short enough for the handtied to sit on top of the vase without tilting to one side. If using glassware, ensure it is clean.
- Remember not to make the collar too large or more flowers will be needed to fill it.

2

chapter 6

Bridal work

Bridal work is one of the most popular areas of floristry design, because it is associated with a lovely occasion and often includes large-scale design possibilities at the reception or place of worship.

The most important piece is often the bride's bouquet, which, more than any other design, should be tailor-made specifically for the person. It does not have to be a traditional cascading shower bouquet, though these do remain popular in the UK alongside rose handtieds.

So many factors should be considered when creating a bridal bouquet; the cut of the dress, the height of the bride and the colour and style of her hair are some important factors. Any attendants' or bridesmaids' designs need to link with the bride and must also be secure, as they will receive heavy handling.

Designing and creating bridal flowers requires a considerable amount of preparation from the initial consultation to the final installation. Due to the perishable nature of fresh materials, they need to be assembled as close as possible to the event so it is important to adhere to timescales.

With careful planning, bridal work is immensely enjoyable and is often an excellent showcase for your design skills.

Calla lily (*Zantedeschia*) buttonhole

Use

Calla lilies have become a popular choice for those wanting an alternative to the rose. They lend a more contemporary look for modern and tropical themes.

Callas last well out of water, which makes them an ideal flower for wired designs. Do not store in a chiller as, like all tropical materials, they prefer room temperature.

Care should be taken when ordering callas because the larger ones are difficult to pin upright and are therefore unsuitable for buttonholes. It is advisable to ask for small callas such as *Zantedeschia* 'Crystal Blush', as used in this design.

The addition of China grass and tree heather gives a variance in texture.

Materials

Flowers and foliage

2 x small calla lilies (*Zantedeschia* 'Crystal Blush')
2 x tree heather (*Erica arborea*)
3 x China grass (*Liriope muscari*)
3 x *Brachyglottis* (*syn. Senecio greyi*) (optional)

Sundries

fine silver binding wire
stem tape
4 x 0.46 mm gauge stub wires
7 x 0.28 mm gauge stub wires

Method

1. Ensure that all materials have been well conditioned before use (see page 192).

2. Single leg mount with a stub wire. The thickness of wire always depends on the weight and amount of materials used (see Chapter 3 for wiring techniques). In this case, 0.28 mm should be sufficient but you may need a slightly heavier wire.

3. Cut the China grass into three lengths. Two lengths of grass will be placed at the back of the design, so ensure they are long enough to be visible. Single leg mount each stem using a fine silver wire such as 0.28 mm gauge. Single leg mount both ends of the third piece of China grass, so you can loop the grass through your design.

4. Stitch wire each ivy leaf using a fine 0.28 mm gauge stub wire then tape using half-width stem tape.

5. Cut one of the calla lily stems to approximately 2 cm (1 in) in length and the other to approximately 4 cm (2 in) in length. Insert a 0.46 mm gauge wire up through the stem into the seedbox of each calla lily. Then pierce another 0.46 mm gauge wire horizontally through the stem approximately 1 cm (½ in) from the bottom.

   Once you have inserted this wire half way through the stem, gently bend each end down to meet the first wire. You should now have three legs to support the calla lily. Gently tape over all three wires, taking care to cover their insertion points.

6. Position the calla lilies next to one another so that the stem ends meet. One flower should be taller than the other. Wrap the fine silver binding wire around once, just below the stems, to bind the stub wires. Add the two stems of China grass behind the calla lilies, allowing each to be visible above the flower.

7. Add the two stems of tree heather, as seen, and bind once to hold in place.

8. Next, place one wired end of the third piece of China grass (which has been wired at both ends) in front of the design and loop the grass around. Place the other wired end at the back of the design. Ensure that the top of the leaf is visible. Bind once to hold.

9. Finally, add the three wired *Brachyglottis* leaves – two at the front and one at the back. Once all wired materials are included, bring the reel wire down vertically alongside all the stems and trim to a short length of about 3 - 4 cm (1 - 2 in). Cover all the stems with stem tape to form one single stem. Trim off the excess wire length and ensure that the end of the stem is sealed completely and that no bare wires are visible.

10. Insert a pearl-headed (or coloured) pin for future attachment.

Bridesmaid's pomander

Use

This pretty, lightweight design is perfect for a very young bridesmaid because it is so easy to carry.

The name 'pomander' is derived from the French *pomme d'ambre* (amber apple). The term was applied to a mixture of herbs and spices, which were combined with scented resin and made into small spheres to be carried to ward off unpleasant odours.

Pomanders tend to be less time consuming to make than fully wired designs though, for security, it is a good idea to insert the top spray of flowers with wire. The sphere may be covered with leaves as illustrated, or with flower heads. Using only one type of flower such as double or single white *Chrysanthemum* looks particularly effective – the latter giving a very summery daisy-like look. Not only is the *Chrysanthemum* less expensive than other options, but it will withstand being out of water. Indeed, small, flat flowers and dense foliage like *Asparagus densiflorus* 'Myersii' help to retain a spherical shape.

An alternative is a patchwork pomander in which different small materials are distributed around the sphere. Sweet-smelling herbs such as common myrtle (*Myrtus communis*) would be particularly lovely.

When making this design, it is wise to use a bouquet stand (or similar), from which the sphere can be hung while inserting the materials. A small-necked vase – upon which the design can sit while you work - would suffice.

This design uses a dry foam holder, because the materials can tolerate being without moisture for a while. Wet foam spheres can be used, but they are of course heavier when soaked and the security of the handle is more vital.

In this design, a hot pink *Dendrobium* has been used against the *Brachyglottis* (Dunedin Group) 'Sunshine' with a little added bear grass (*Xerophyllum tenax*) for contrast of form.

Materials

Flowers and foliage

25 x stems *Brachyglottis* (Dunedin Group) 'Sunshine' leaves
2 x stems Singapore orchid (*Dendrobium*)
6 x strands of bear grass (*Xerophyllum tenax*)

Sundries

0.5 m (2 ft) pink organza ribbon (for handle)
dry foam sphere
silver stub wires (0.28 mm and 0.46 mm)
long 0.71 mm stub wire
white or green stem tape
cold glue

Tip

Always work towards yourself when placing materials in this way (this is often called basing), because each leaf tip will partially overlap the base of the one before.

Alternative flowers and foliage

Flowers

Phalaenopsis orchids, spray roses, lily-of-the-valley (*Convallaria*), *Amaranthus*, *Stephanotis*, jasmine trails.

Foliage

Lambs' ears (*Stachys lanata*) - fresh or freeze dried, *Elaeaegnus pungens*, or for a rich deep crimson colour, smoke bush (*Cotinus*) leaves.

Note - the softer and more pliable the leaf, the better. This does not apply to young leaves in the spring, though, which will shrivel too quickly.

Method

1. Cut the ribbon to a length of approximately 25 cm (10 in) for the handle. Using a heavy silver wire (0.46 mm), mount both ends of the ribbon together.

2. Tape the ends of the wire using the white or green half-width stem tape. Then tape these to a stronger, long 0.71 mm wire. This will now be long and strong enough to push through the foam sphere. Once it has appeared at the other end, return the remainder of the wire back into the foam for security.

3. Sort the leaves into uniform sizes – leaves that are too big or too small will look visually uneven. Place the leaves on the work surface with the back facing upwards. Place a small amount of cold florists' glue all over the back of each leaf. Do eight leaves at a time and wait for about 30 seconds for the glue to go slightly tacky. This makes them stick more easily.

4. Starting at the handle, work out a preferred pattern for the leaves. Place the first leaf on the foam and press down gently until it has stuck firmly. Carry on sticking the other leaves to the foam working in lines to achieve a neat pattern. Once one line is complete, start the next line, slightly overlapping the leaves to avoid any gaps in the foam.

5. Once you have completely covered the sphere with leaves, prepare the orchids by wiring them with silver wires and fashioning into small branching units (see page 35). Insert them into the top of the sphere at the base of the handle, and further secure with a decorative pearl-headed pin.

6. Store in a cool place, but avoid misting directly onto the orchids or ribbon – cover the pomander with tissue and spray the air above it instead.

2

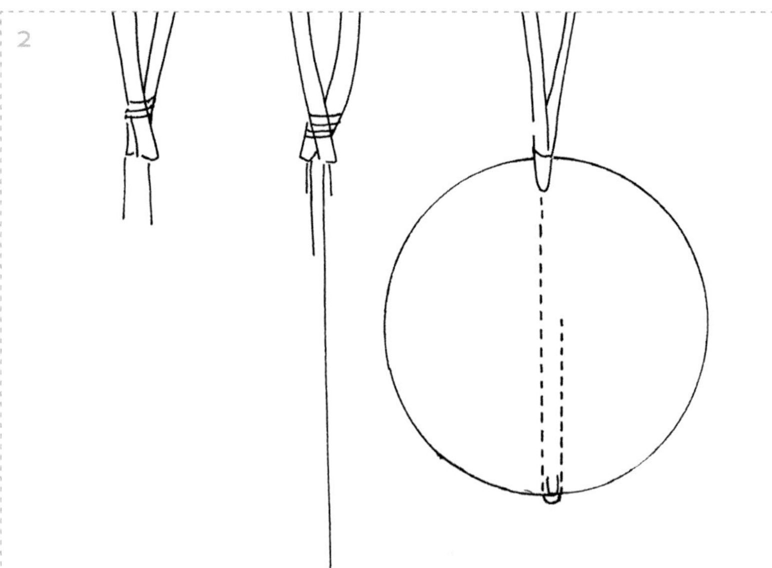

4

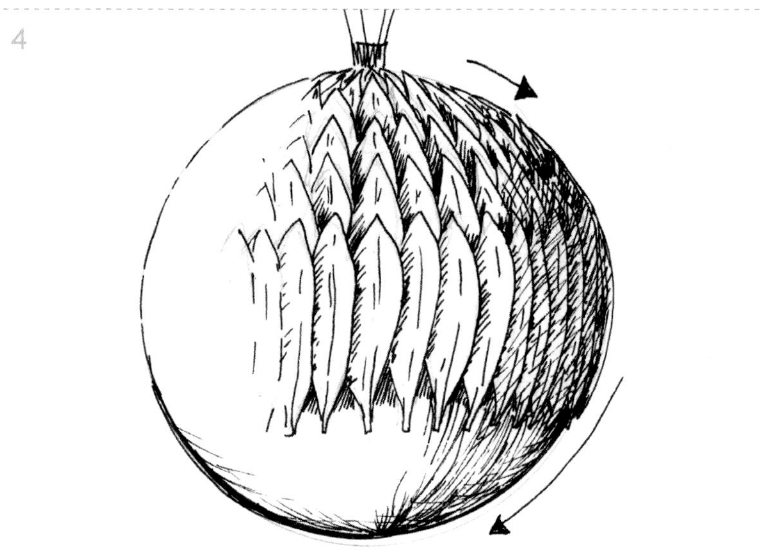

4

Basket arrangement

Use

Basket arrangements are very versatile – they are appropriate for a bridesmaid to carry at a wedding, or simply to decorate the home.

Baskets lend themselves to fresh flowers and foliage due to their natural appearance. For centuries, flowers have been placed in baskets: from the harvesting trug to the many different shapes now available.

This design has been made for a bridesmaid to carry at a summer wedding. The trailing ivy (*Hedera helix*) gives a country-like feel and peonies (*Paeonia*) give impact.

Materials

Flowers and foliage

5 x pink *Paeonia lactiflora* 'Sarah Bernhardt'
6 x trails *Hedera helix*
8 x brodiaea (*Triteleia*)
8 x quaking grass (*Briza media*)

Sundries

$^{1}/_{3}$ brick of wet floral foam
low-sided, open-weave basket no larger than 20 cm (8 in)
2 x long 0.90 mm gauge wires
stem tape
pot tape

2

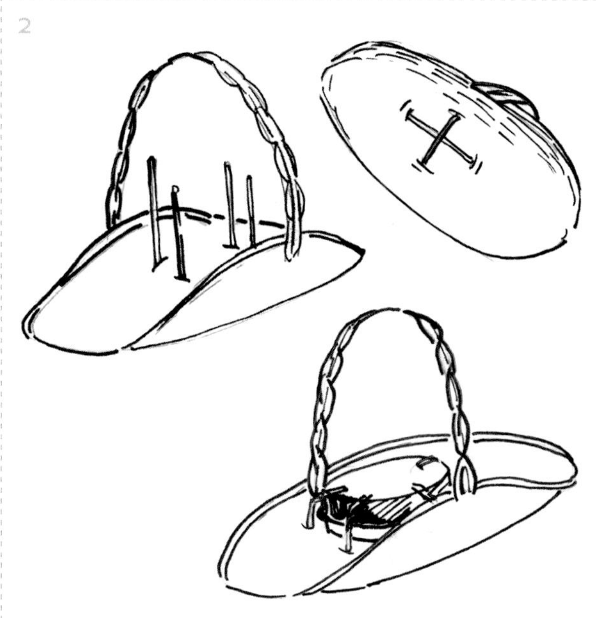

3

Method

1. Cut one third from a brick of foam and soak. Place in a plastic container and secure using the pot tape.

2. Tape two long 0.90 mm gauge stub wires together with green stem tape and insert through the weave in the base of the basket (from underneath). Place the prepared container in the centre of the basket. Bring each end of wire up over the container's rim and bend over to secure. This is a very neat, unobtrusive method of securing the mechanics, which is particularly important since it is being carried at a wedding.

3. Insert the foliage outline following the basic oval shape of the basket. Remember to allow 3 – 4 cm (1 – 2 in) of clean stem at the base of each, so that the foliage can be inserted into the foam securely.

4. Add the focal flowers (in this design, the peonies, by virtue of their size and form). Place the central flower directly below the handle and the next two either side, slightly lower down and at a slight diagonal angle to each other.

Tips

To link the colour of the bridesmaids' dresses, ribbon can be twisted around the handle or satin bows tied to its base of the handle. The basket could also be prepared this way if being used to hold rose petals for throwing.

4

Alternative flowers and foliage

Flowers

Roses, veronica (*Hebe*), *Freesia*, lisianthus (*Eustoma*), *Ixia*, *Astilbe*, sweet William (*Dianthus barbatus*), *Bouvardia*.

Foliage

Eucalyptus 'Baby Blue', bear grass (*Xerophyllum tenax*), soft ruscus (*Danae racemosa*).

Bridal orb

Use

This unconventional bridal bouquet is designed to sit comfortably in the palm of the hand. It should be held at waist height, or wherever feels most comfortable.

A bridal orb can look soft and flowing with the use of ivy (*Hedera*) trails, *Amaranthus* or *Asparagus setaceus*. The middle finger can be slipped through a loop at the base to hold it securely. The illustrated design uses the soft felt-like *Stachys lanata* leaves to cover the sphere, though fabric would cover equally well.

Polystyrene spheres are ideal to use as they are much cleaner than florists' foam and do not spill dust when cut. These are, however, quite difficult to source in the UK (though readily available in Holland, Belgium and Germany), so foam is the best alternative.

Method

1. Cut a wedge out of the top section of the dry foam sphere. Cut a similar wedge out of wet foam, which should be lightly soaked and inserted into the dry foam gap. Secure with cocktail sticks or large wire hairpins. For extra security, place hot glue on the dry foam before inserting the wet foam wedge.

2. Cover the 0.90 mm stub wire with stem tape. Make a small loop at one end of the wire. Twist the wire under the loop to secure. Push the wire through the base of the sphere, all the way through, and out of the top. Bend and return the wire end back into the sphere to secure.

3. Use the cold glue to attach the leaves to the foam. Lay the leaves on a flat surface and lightly coat the underside of each with cold glue. Wait one minute for the glue to go slightly tacky. If the leaves are done in small batches of about 10, by the time the first five are placed onto the foam, the next batch will be tacky. As an alternative, the leaves could be attached using pearl-headed or diamanté pins to give a decorative look.

4. Carefully position the leaves working towards you; the base of the previous leaf should be slightly overlapped by the tip of the next until the whole sphere is covered. Ensure that the wet foam remains uncovered. A neat pattern is best, but the security of the workmanship is - as always - the most important feature.

5. Once the sphere is complete, place the flowers into the top of the exposed wet foam. Insert the foliage following the curve of the sphere, then add the flowers. Orchids are ideal as they are a flat form and will therefore sit well on top of the sphere. These will need to be support wired (see Chapter 3).

6. To store, place the sphere on top of a small vase, which will give support. Lightly cover with tissue paper.

Materials

Flowers and foliage

40 - 50 x *Stachys* leaves (these were in fact freeze dried but fresh leaves work just as well).
2 x *Phalaenopsis* orchid heads (house plant orchids have smaller heads than cut ones and are often less expensive)
2 x stems *Juniperus*
2 x small stems corkscrew hazel (*Corylus avellana*)

Sundries

dry foam sphere 9 or 12 cm (3 or 4 in)
small wedge of foam (wet)
cold glue
1 heavy long stub wire 0.90 mm gauge
stem tape
cocktail sticks or 0.90 mm wires
hot glue gun

4

Tip

Although orchids benefit from a light spray, never spray furry leaves such as *Stachys* as they will loose their grey colour. They will also absorb too much water and become sodden and unattractive. Spray the orchids before they are placed onto the sphere if necessary.

Circlet headdress

Use

This classic circular band of flowers is traditionally worn by young bridesmaids. It is a pretty and feminine design rather than grown-up and elegant.

When selecting flowers, remember that a lot of body heat is emitted from the head and that the wired flowers will be out of water for several hours. Therefore, care should be taken to select suitable flowers; the lasting quality of flowers in a wired design is of the utmost importance. If you are unsure about the suitability of any fresh material, it is a good idea to cut, wire and leave it overnight to see how it fares.

The featured design includes *Chrysanthemum* as it is long lasting. We should not be dismissive of using chrysanthemums - over the years the Dutch growers have developed many attractive small-headed varieties that lend themselves to wedding designs. Their daisy-like appearance looks summery in pale colours but looks equally good in autumn and winter in rich dark red and orange tones.

Materials

Flowers and foliage

4 x stems yellow *Chrysanthemum* 'Santini'
7 x stems veronica (*Hebe*) - dark red foliage will contrast well with the *Chrysanthemum*

Sundries

fine silver stub wires (0.28 mm gauge)
2 x heavier wires for frame (0.71 mm gauge)
green stem tape
satin ribbon (optional)
florists' scissors and sharp fabric scissors (to cut ribbon)

Tip

It is quicker to first wire all materials then tape them rather than stopping and starting both jobs.

Alternative materials

Dendrobium orchids, spray carnation (*Dianthus*), *Gypsophila*, small headed *Chrysanthemum*, sweet William (*Dianthus barbatus*), *Scabiosa*, *Astilbe* florets, *Agapanthus* florets, range of small-scale foliages such as *Hebe*, *Euonymus*.

Flowers to avoid

We are often misled by attractive photographs that show unsuitable materials, which would not last and are only good for photoshoots. The following flowers would not survive out of water:

- sweet peas (*Lathyrus odoratus*)
- most spring flowers including anemones
- veronica (*Hebe*)
- *Bouvardia*

There are however some compromises that can be made. Small, delicate spray roses often wilt overnight but these could be pre-wired, left un-taped in a glass of water and simply taped up the next morning and included into the design nearer to the event.

Method

1. Ensure that you have conditioned all materials well. In warm weather, materials taken from the garden should be cut in the cool of the evening or early morning, and then immediately placed in water to drink. Purchased flowers should always be re-cut and placed in tepid, clean water for a long drink (minimum of three hours).

2. Once conditioned, cut the stems of the *Chrysanthemum* and *Hebe* short - approximately 3 cm (1 in) - prior to wiring.

3. Single leg mount wire all materials into small bunches of two or three stems, depending on how wide you wish the headdress to look. Generally, for small bridesmaids the band should not be too thick. A double leg mount is not necessary as the wire is being taped very close to the stem and any excess weight should be avoided.

4. Once you have wired all the materials, begin taping. Cut the tape to half its reel width, which also reduces bulk. The circlet should have a degree of flexibility, to enable it to be moulded onto the head effectively.

5. Prepare the circular base by taping two 0.71 mm gauge stub wires individually. If you need extra length, tape one to the other with a slight overlap where the two join together. Depending on the colours of your flower materials, green, white or even brown stem tape can be used. Bend the wire into a circular shape. Then bend each end of the wire into a hook so that they will lock together.

6. Still using the half-width tape, place either a *Chrysanthemum* or *Hebe* bunch onto the pre-formed circle and attach by taping firmly. Ensure you pull the tape securely.

7. Continue to alternate these bunches until you have covered the whole circle. If desired, make a bow to adorn it. This can be a good way to link in the colour of the bridesmaids' dresses.

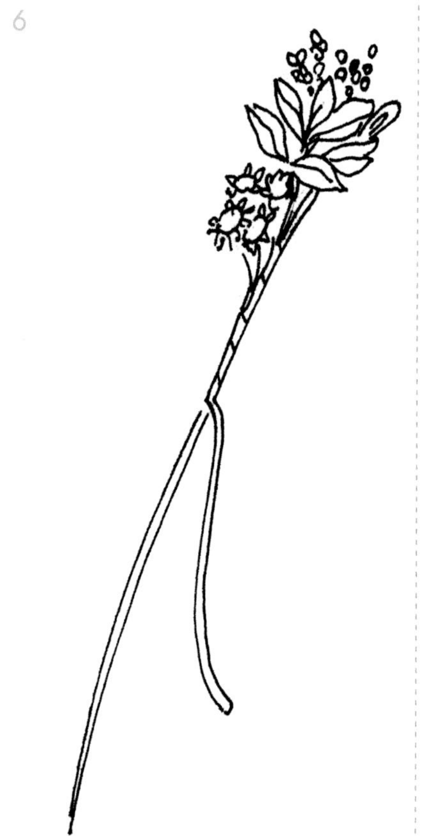
6

7

Classic shower bouquet

Use

This classic style of bouquet, which uses cascading flowers and foliage, is a popular choice for many brides. Created in a foam holder, it has a symmetrical shape and a sumptuous and romantic feel.

The overall shape is gently rounded at the top, and the centre of the top half is emphasised. The lower part of the design consists of flowers and foliage, which appear to cascade from the central point.

The style can vary slightly according to the bride's dress and theme. The wilder country look, with lots of open roses and trailing ivy, is ideal for a full-skirted dress. A more tailored, elegant look can be created by using oriental lilies and *Stephanotis* trails.

It is important to pay attention to the profile of the bouquet as much as the front. A flat bouquet will look unsightly. A good profile can be achieved by ensuring the materials at the top are slightly angled back over the handle of the bouquet holder.

It is also essential that construction is neat and secure, as the bouquet will have a lot of handling. All longer lower materials should be mount wired before inserting into the foam (see page 34). The bouquet should still have plenty of natural movement and not appear too rigid.

Materials

Flowers and foliage

7 x *Rosa* 'Akito' or other small white roses
5 x lisianthus (*Eustoma* 'Picolo')
5 x *Nephrolepis exaltata* fern
7 x variegated ivy (*Hedera*) trails
7 x *Phlox*
4 x *Dracaena deremensis* leaves
small filler foliage such as *Hebe* or *Euonymus*
3 x stems grasses such as fountain grass (*Panicum*)

Sundries

foam bouquet holder
double-sided tape
about 2 m (6 ½ ft) cord
0.71 or 0.90 mm stub wires (depending on weight of the roses)
1 large pearl bead
hot glue gun
bouquet stand

Tip

To protect the handle from getting dirty as you work, cover with cling film or a plastic bag secured with a rubber band.

Alternative flowers and foliage

Focal flowers – oriental lilies, longiflorum lilies (*Lilium longiflorum*), calla lilies (*Zantedeschia*), *Cymbidium* orchids.
Transitional materials – *Freesia, Convallaria, Stephanotis, Bouvardia, Astrantia, Astilbe, Scabiosa, Dendrobium, Ixia*, spray carnation, bridal gladioli (*Gladiolus colvillii*), spray roses.
Outline foliage – soft ruscus (*Danae racemosa*), *Nephrolepis* fern, *Eucalyptus* 'Baby Blue'.

Method

1. Prepare the handle by completely covering the white plastic with double-sided sticky tape, which enables the decorative cord or ribbon to adhere easily to the handle without unravelling. Begin at the bottom of the handle and wrap the cord around it tightly and neatly until it reaches the very top of the holder, which widens out.

2. Secure the ends with a small dab of hot melt glue. For a decorative finish, the single pearl can be placed at the bottom of the handle.

3. Lightly spray the foam holder with water. Avoid soaking completely, because this will make it heavy and also cause excess water to drip down the handle as stems are inserted. Place the holder in a bouquet stand.

4. Begin by placing an outline of foliage in a pear shape on the outside edge of the foam.

   Remember to angle some of the top pieces backwards over the top of the handle to create a three-dimensional profile. Leave the centre of the foam empty to allow for flower stems to be inserted. You can fill in any gaps when all the flowers are in place.

5. Place the central rose directly in the centre of the plastic circle on the foam holder (this draws the eye to the focal area). This stem should be internally support wired using a 0.71 or 0.90 mm gauge wire, depending on the weight of the rose. For extra security, put a small dab of hot glue on the end of the stem just before inserting it into the foam.

6. Position two other roses low into the foam diagonally opposite the centre rose. Place the other roses in a 'lazy S' pattern above and below the three central roses.

7. Ensure that all roses placed below the central one are single leg mounted on a 0.71 or 0.90 mm gauge wire. For each, return the long wire back into the foam, which will prevent the roses from falling out. The stem end should be inserted into the foam so that it has a source of water. At this point, any decorative foliage could be added to the centre - such as the rolled *Dracaena* leaves in the picture.

8. Place the secondary or transitional flowers (such as the *Eustoma*) in a diagonal grouping through the design, from the top left to the lower right. Remember to angle these materials slightly back over the top of the holder for a good profile. Ensure there are at least two recessed flowers in the centre and that the outer stems are long enough to give a flowing appearance and good outline shape.

9. Add the next transitional flowers (such as the *Phlox*) in a second diagonal grouping from the top right to the lower left. This should complete the flower placements.

10. Fill in any gaps where the foam may be visible with small pieces of foliage. Lightly mist and protect the bouquet with a piece of tissue paper draped over the top. Store in a cool place.

1

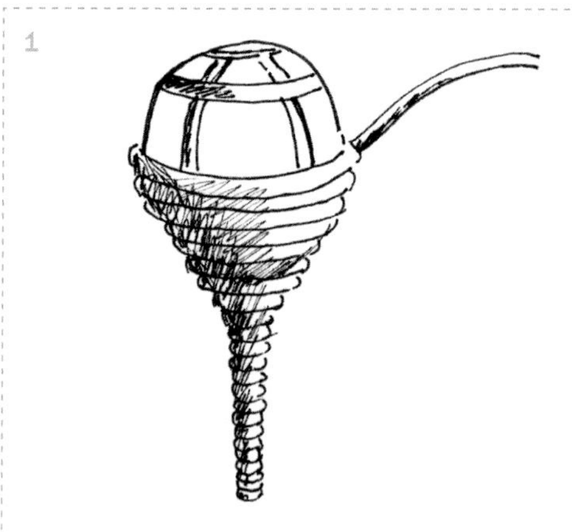

4

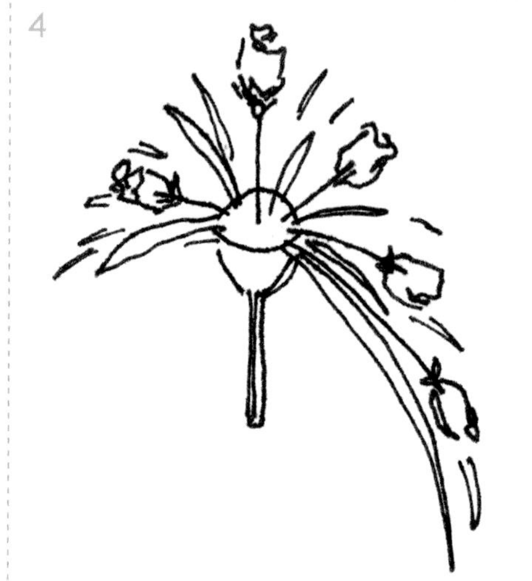

5

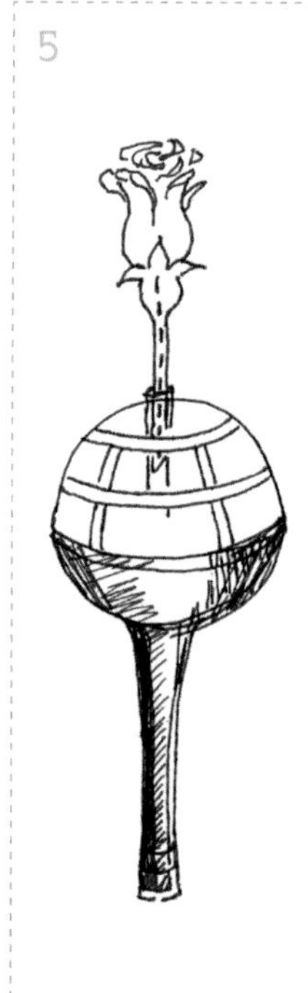

6

Tied posy for a bridesmaid

Use

In recent years, the tied posy has probably been the most popular design for both bridesmaids and brides. It is a very pretty design that encapsulates the notion of informally-picked flowers from the meadow.

The same technique can also be used to create exotic and modern-looking handtieds with the use of calla lilies (*Zantedeschia*) and bear grass (*Xerophyllum tenax*) amongst many others.

The key to achieving success with this design is to master the spiralling stem technique, which creates a voluminous shape.

Handtieds for bridesmaids should be small scale and not cumbersome to hold. This example contains the ever-popular sweet pea (*Lathyrus odoratus*). Using sweet peas for weddings is usually not encouraged due to their short-lasting qualities, but a handtied design will allow the flowers to be in water for as long as possible before the event.

Materials

Flowers and foliage

10 x sweet peas (*Lathyrus odoratus*)
10 x *Triteleia*
5 x *Phlox*
5 x spray roses
5 x *Chrysanthemum* 'Santini'

Sundries

twine, raffia, paper covered wire or polypropylene ribbon to tie
2 m (6½ ft) decorative ribbon to finish

Tips

- Covering the stems with stem tape (preferably white if using pale ribbon) will keep them straight and help the ribbon to wrap around them more securely.
- If the design is made in advance of the occasion (which is advisable), leave the posy overnight in an appropriate size vase that will not damage the flowers. Gently and loosely wrap it with tissue paper to protect the blooms.

Alternative flowers

Small tied posies need smaller scale flower materials such as the following:

Summer - sweet William (*Dianthus barbatus*), veronica (*Hebe*), *Scabiosa, Centaurea, Campanula, Astilbe, Eryngium planum.*

Spring - *Bouvardia, Calendula, Narcissus, Ranunculus, Triteleia, Anemone, Celosia caracas.*

Autumn / winter – *Carthamus, Tanacetum*, roses, *Asclepias, Crocosmia.*

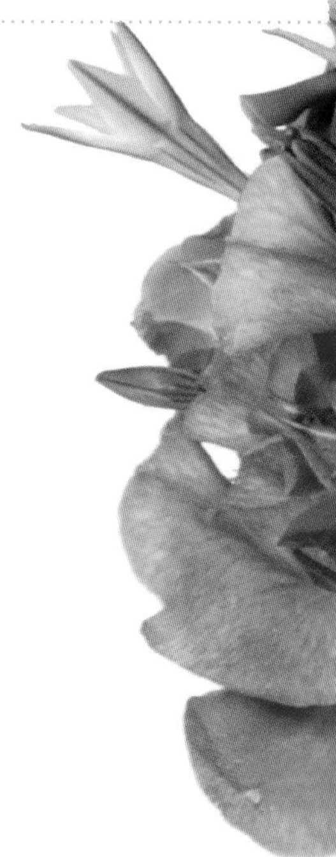

Method

1. Defoliate each stem to the very top. This must be done at this stage, because clean stems are a feature of this design. Use a plastic rose stripper or a florists' knife to de-thorn the roses.

2. Follow the basic handtied method described on page 66.

3. Trim the stems fairly short, usually no more than 20 cm (8 in). You can leave the stems exposed - as illustrated - or bind with stem tape to hold them together. Cover with a wide satin ribbon and secure with pearl-headed pins.

1

2

2

Cake top

Materials

Flowers and foliage

5 x yellow roses
1 stem mimosa (*Acacia dealbata*)
6 - 8 x short ivy (*Hedera*) trails
(a pot plant is ideal)
3 - 5 x filler foliage such as *Hebe*
or *Euonymus*

Sundries

white aerosol can top
floral foam
pot tape

Use

This is a simple but effective round design for the top tier of a wedding cake. It could also be used at other notable occasions such as a Christening or anniversary celebration.

It is important to have some material cascading gently over the sides of the container and the cake. This design uses yellow roses and mimosa making it ideal for a spring wedding. The container should be small. White lids from aerosol cans are the perfect vessel.
However if the bride wants a more slender container it may be necessary to wire the flowers in a posy style construction so that the wired stem can be inserted into the container. This will, of course, take longer to construct than this illustrated design which is made in florists' foam.

3

6

Tip

Care should be taken to avoid using toxic or irritant materials on cakes. Ivy is poisonous but only if ingested. So providing the cake top is removed from the cake prior to cutting ivy is acceptable. Sappy materials and berries should be avoided.

Method

1. Cut a small piece of foam to fit the aerosol container allowing a small amount of foam to sit above the top of the container. Soak the foam.

2. Secure the foam in the container with pot tape.

3. Insert short stems of ivy about 10 cm (4 in) long into the edge of the foam, on a slight angle upwards so they cascade over the edge of the container.

4. Place a rose centrally in the foam. This should be approximately 10 cm (4 in) tall once inserted.

5. Position two more roses either side, at slightly different lengths and on a slight angle.

6. Add the remaining two roses throughout the design.

7. Reinforce the outline shape by placing about five 10 cm (4 in) lengths of foliage on the outer edges of the design. Add some small pieces to the centre on a slight angle so that they appear to radiate from the centre.

8. Add the filler foliage such as the *Hebe* to cover any visible foam. Lightly spray and store in a cool place until required.

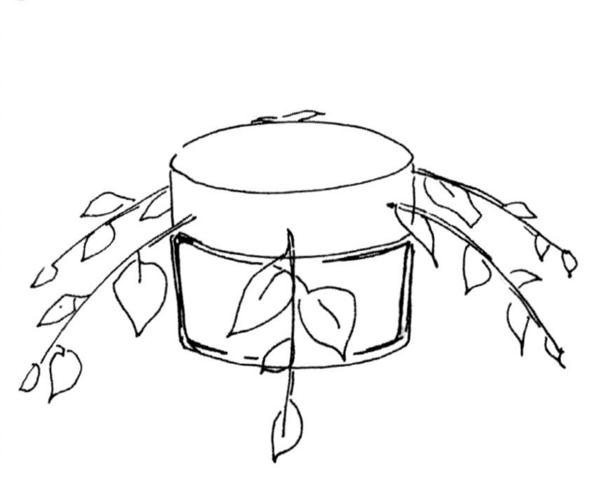

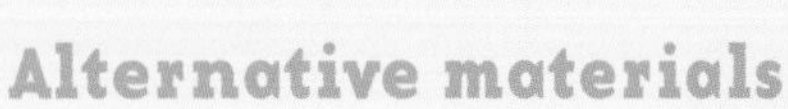

Alternative materials

Spray roses, golden rod (*Solidago*), *Gypsophila*, broom (*Genista*), September flower *Aster* ericoides.

chapter 7

Sympathy designs

Flowers convey emotion and there is no more emotive time than the death of a loved one. Funerals are the last opportunity to say goodbye and to celebrate the life of a person - who they were, what they did and how they touched others' lives.

When words are difficult to convey, flowers can express so much – particularly if made with that person's favourite blooms, or depicting something that was pertinent to them in the form of a floral symbol or logo.

The design should be as bespoke as wedding flowers and reflect the character of the deceased, their life and what they meant to those around them. There are many considerations when selecting the style of design and type of flower and foliage.

The formal details need to be confirmed – the day, date and time of the funeral. The flowers are usually taken to the funeral directors, but sometimes they go to the church or wherever the service is being held. If the tribute is to be placed on the coffin, accommodate the height restriction imposed by the hearse. Popular design shapes have different meanings. Hearts are generally associated with a close family member or friend, whilst the cross has a strong religious association. Solid posy pads, pillows and cushions are good shapes for basing flowers or layering leaves to create a formal tribute. The circular wreath is perhaps the most well known of all tributes, symbolising everlasting life. It is a mistake, though, to assume that when someone asks for a wreath they do actually mean the classic round circle. More often than not, further discussion reveals that they actually want something quite different; the term 'wreath' is widely used for all funeral flowers.

Floral letters have been popularised commercially and though they can be made personal, they are not the prettiest of the wide range of tributes on offer. It is up to the florist to explain the range of designs available.

This chapter shows some of the most commercially popular designs and gives examples of both formal and informal designs, including a based and natural twig wreath, a classic coffin spray and mixed open tributes.

Based wreath

Use

Based designs are often, though not always, sent to a close family member.

The technique of basing (placing flowers close together with no space in between) is still widely used in commercially popular funeral designs. Using flowers tightly massed in this way enhances the outline shape of a design to its optimum.

Basing is ideal for open or solid shapes such as a heart, chaplet, wreath, posy pad, or cross. It gives a much more formal look to the design.

Remember that using this massed technique requires a large quantity of materials for even a modest size wreath. This is why *Chrysanthemum* are widely used rather than the more expensive carnations. Blooms should be at their optimum and be as open as possible in order to give maximum coverage.

The illustrated design is on a 30 cm (12 in) wreath frame edged with polypropylene ribbon. Alternatively, you can use single leaves but this would add to the time and therefore cost, as every leaf would need to be stitched with wire to give both flexibility and security. A small spray of flowers is added to complete the design. This should link to the colour of the edging as much as possible. Many people do not like using ribbon, but there are so many different types to choose between, all creating a certain look. Delicate net ribbon could be used to suggest a ballerina's tutu; tartan for Scottish connections; or hessian for a rustic look. Take care to select ribbons that withstand moisture.

Materials

Flowers and foliage

20 - 25 x stems white double *Chrysanthemum*
1 stem pink lily
2 x soft ruscus (*Danae racemosa*) foliage
4 x stems wax flower (*Chamelaucium*)
a few stems of heather (*Erica*)
conifer

Sundries

30 cm (12 in) wreath frame
small square of foam for the spray or OASIS 'Le Bump'®
pins (for attachment of the ribbon edge)
stapler (for making the pleated ribbon edge)
pot tape
florists' knife and scissors

Method

1. Tape a small piece of foam to the top of the ring with pot tape. Alternatively screw on a Le Bump OASIS®.

2. Soak the foam frame (with attachment) by placing it face down in deep water. Avoid over soaking. The process should take approximately one minute.

3. Prepare the ribbon pleating by folding the ribbon, then bringing in another pleat to meet it. The whole pleat should be no wider than 5 cm (2 in), so each half pleat is approximately 2.5 cm (1 in).

4. Repeat this process until you have sufficient length to edge the frame outside and inside.

5. Slightly chamfer (cut away) the edge of the wet foam using a florists' knife.

6. Before positioning the pleated ribbon on the inside edge, gently tear the ribbon's outer edge to narrow the overall width. This will maintain the circle in the centre.

7. Attach by pinning the pleated ribbon at the top edge, where the staples are positioned. Ensure that the pins go into the hard foam at the base of the wreath (usually paler green in colour).

8. Cut the *Chrysanthemum* flower heads off fairly short – though not too short. This allows for the central flowers on top of the frame to be slightly taller and will give a slightly bevelled profile instead of a completely flat one.

9. Start by placing the slightly smaller *Chrysanthemum* heads around the outside edge of the frame making sure there are no foam gaps between the flowers and the ribbon edge. Ideally, the flower heads should disguise the pins.

10. Do the same on the inside of the frame, then fill another row above each of these two outer rows. Ideally, there should be odd rows so that there is one single row running centrally on top of the frame. As most varieties of *Chrysanthemum* are not voluminous, it normally takes five rows rather than three.

11. Once you have completely covered the foam with *Chrysanthemum*, complete the spray. Start by making an outline edge of foliage. It is good practice to follow the curve of the wreath frame. The two outer edges of foliage should be slightly longer than the rest to give a crescent shape.

12. Place the open focal flower (the lily in the illustrated design) in the centre. Either side of this central flower, place two less open lily heads, and recess them slightly.

13. Add the smaller, transitional flowers in a diagonal pattern through the design. Angle the stems to create the impression that the materials are radiating from the central point. As the spray is small scale, cut the stems quite short, so that the spray does not engulf the wreath frame.

14. Lightly mist the design and store it in a cool place.

1

10

Tips

- Double *Chrysanthemum* tend to sit together better than single ones, and give a stronger density to the overall design.
- When buying double *Chrysanthemum* for basing, ensure they are good quality, because they can shatter easily.
- During winter, *Chrysanthemum* heads can be slightly smaller, so more stems will be required to complete the design.

Flower quantities for different sized tributes

20 cm (8 in) based wreath you will need 15 stems spray *Chrysanthemum*
25 cm (10 in) based wreath you will need 20 stems spray *Chrysanthemum*
35 cm (14 in) based wreath you will need 30 stems spray *Chrysanthemum*

Tied sheaf

Use

Sheaves are considered an informal funeral tribute and can be made to look classically elegant, rustic or simply seasonal. They should not be wrapped. Due to their informality, sheaves are ideal for someone such as a work colleague or neighbour.

Tied sheaves are designed to have a flat back and they work well when laid on the ground. The spiralled stems are key to the design's success and a good profile should be achieved at the focal area by the angling of the stems during construction.

2

Materials

Flowers and foliage

3 x stems laurel (*Prunus laurocerasus*)
3 x stems kentia palm (*Howea forsteriana*)
8 x stems Easter lilies (*Lilium longiflorum*)
3 x aralia (*Fatsia japonica*) leaves
3 x *Aspidistra*
½ bunch fountain grass (*Panicum*)

Alternative flowers and foliage

Some longer-stemmed flowers are needed to get the required height at the top of the design.

Focal flowers – roses (larger varieties such as white 'Avalanche', yellow 'Sphinx', pink 'Esperance', peach 'Sweet Avalanche'), sunflower (*Helianthus*), large *Gerbera*, *Agapanthus*.

Transitional flowers – standard and spray *Dianthus*, tulips, *Liatris*, *Aconitum*, lisianthus (*Eustoma*), *Alstroemeria*, *Astilbe*, statice (*Limonium*).

Foliage for the base collar – elephants' ears (*Bergenia*), *Philodendron*, *Aspidistra* (can be rolled), *Helleborus* leaves.

Method

1. Defoliate the flower stems to half way.

2. Take the tallest and straightest piece of foliage and add two pieces, slightly shorter in length, either side. Initially, these three stems will cross, but as you add more materials to the left side, it is important to place them on top of each other, and all materials you add to the right side should have their stems tucked under each other. This way, the stems will spiral. Angling the stems will ensure that a good profile is achieved.

3. Place the longest flower material at the top and create a 'lazy S' of focal - or impact - flowers through the centre of the design (if using mixed flowers).

4. Add transitional flowers to form a diagonal grouping. Follow the same method of placing the left-side flowers with their stems on top, and right-side flowers with their stem beneath. Add fountain grass if available.

5. When the last flowers are placed at the base of the design, finish by adding three large leaves, such as *Fatsia*, to form a collar at the base. These need to be stitch wired using a long green 0.71 mm gauge wire (see page 40).

6. Add a modest bow under the leaves in a toning colour. Tidy the stem ends by cutting.

Tips

- Try to select flower materials that will tolerate being out of water - such as lilies, *Chrysanthemum* or carnations - particularly if the weather is warm.
- A backing of foliage helps to build a good structure.
- The design does not need to be held aloft, as this can be tiring on the arm. If placing on a work bench, ensure the binding point is not resting on the surface. This way, stems can be angled towards the floor to give an elevated profile.
- Keep in water until delivery or collection.

Open cross

Use

The open cross is generally a more formal tribute and is traditionally placed on the coffin.

The cross is the Christian symbol, derived from the crucifixion of Christ. It has given way to softer, more flowing coffin sprays. Modern designs could include dogwood (*Cornus*) or bamboo (*Bambusa*) as alternative foundations.

This design shows an open cross with a foliage edging. Open funeral tributes are informal and use mixed flowers and foliage on the base with some space in between rather than tightly packed flowers and/or foliage. The colour choice in this illustration suggests a more feminine tribute.

As with most foam tributes, there are several sizes available, but 30 cm (12 in) and 35 cm (14 in) tend to be the most widely used.

Materials

Flowers and foliage

8 x peach roses
about 12 stems of filler foliage such as *Euonymus*, small-leaved-*Hebe* or myrtle (*Myrtus communis*)
10 x stems of transitional flower such as *Papaver seedheads* (used here) or *Rudbeckia* seedheads, *Hydrangea* or spray carnation (*Dianthus*)
about 40 short pieces of x *Cuprocyparis leylandii* or leather leaf (*Arachnoides*) foliage for edging
about 6 stems of a contrasting soft form such as *Briza* grass (used here)

Sundries

1 cross frame 30 cm (12 in)

Tips

To save time, avoid using single leaves for the edging which require individual wiring. Choose foliage that has a stiff stem that can be inserted straight into the foam.

If foliage is hard to obtain for the edging, use ribbon instead. Hessian ribbon would work well with this design.

Ensure there are some filler foliages for the top such as *Hebe*, *Euonymus* or ming fern, as they will be needed to cover the foam.

Alternative flowers and foliage

Focal flowers – small sunflowers (*Helianthus*), *Dahlia*, Asiatic lilies, *Iris*, germini.

Transitional flowers – *Asclepias*, *Chrysanthemum* 'Santini', *Freesia*, *Crocosmia.*

Filler materials – *Hydrangea* florets, sea holly (*Eryngium*).

Foliage edging – hard ruscus (*Ruscus hypophyllum*), single leaves such as *Galax* or ivy (*Hedera*).

Method

1. Soak the foam cross by placing it with the top face down in a sink or bath. If unavailable hold under a tap until fully soaked.

2. Prepare foliage for the edging by defoliating the lower fronds so that approximately 5 cm (2 in) of clean stem can be inserted into the foam. Push each stem slightly upwards - on a diagonal rather than horizontal angle - into the edge of the lower part of the wet foam. This way a much more effective pattern is achieved. Always work towards you so that the tip of the current foliage slightly overlaps the one before it.

3. Once the edge is complete, place the focal roses on top of the cross. These are positioned vertically. The central group of roses can be placed first, followed by one at the top and another at the base of the long arm.

4. Position the other roses throughout the design.

5. Next, use any transitional materials and small-scale filler foliage such as *Hebe*, *Euonymus* or ming (*Asparagus umbellatus*) fern to fill the gaps.

6. Lightly spray and store in a cool place until required.

2

3

4

Open heart

Use

This would be a suitable tribute for a close family member or friend. The open nature of the flower placements is less formal than that of a based heart.

This design follows a similar method to the open cross, as the flower materials are mixed with some space in between rather than solidly massed together to form a uniform surface.

This heart features an alternative edging to the mixed foliage in the cross by using a flexible thin bark on hessian. An alternative to this would be a hessian ribbon.

Materials

Flowers and foliage

8 x orange roses
7 x stems *Hypericum*
5 x stems birch (*Betula pendula*)
8 x stems *Rudbeckia*
2 x stems ming fern (*Asparagus umbellatus*)
2 x stems juniper *Juniperus*

Sundries

open heart frame 30 cm (12 in). Do not use a frame with a hard plastic base, but one with a hard foam base into which pins can be inserted.
about 2 m (6½ ft) hessian-backed bark
straight pins

4

4

4

Method

1. Soak the heart frame by placing it face down in a sink or bucket of water.

2. Pin the bark edging onto the sides of the open heart.

3. Cut some of the foliage short, to about 6 cm (2½ in), ensuring that the lower stem is defoliated. Place in an evenly distributed pattern on top of the frame until partially covered.

4. Insert the roses equal distances apart, in the shape of the heart. These will be the focal flowers as they give strong impact (and are also the most expensive). Place them slightly higher than the rest of the materials.

5. Intersperse the *Rudbeckia* between the roses at a slightly lower level. Fill in with the *Hypericum* berries. The slightly differing lengths of the materials will give the design depth and added interest and prevent it from looking monotonous by pulling the eye in and out of the design.

6. Add a few stems of the *Betula* twig over the top of the design to add extra volume and space. Insert the lower end of the stem into the foam. Double leg mount wire the softer tips using a 0.56 mm gauge stub wire (see chapter 3) as this will help keep the twigs in place.

7. Lightly mist the design and store in a cool place.

Tip

Ensure the inside edging is kept as close as possible to the frame to retain the heart shape inside.

Alternative materials

Focal flowers – tulips, *Iris*, Asiatic lilies, small sunflowers, dahlias.
Transitional flowers – *Freesia*, spray carnations, *Alstroemeria*, *Chrysanthemum* 'Santini', lisianthus (*Eustoma*).

Coffin spray

Use

If one impressive floral tribute from all family members - rather than several smaller ones - is chosen, a coffin spray is ideal. It is, therefore, a very significant and important design.

A coffin spray is a very effective way of softening the coffin's appearance - particularly if trailing materials are used such as *Euphorbia fulgens*, long-stemmed French tulips and soft ruscus. The overall shape is that of a diamond viewed from above, though this is softened by the placement of long, flowing materials around the outline.

Coffin sprays can be made to a considerable length, but it is important to remember that the height between the top of the coffin and the roof of the hearse is 23 cm (9 in). If the height of the flowers exceeds this, they will be knocked off. Generally, coffin sprays should be two-thirds the length of the coffin. With wicker coffins, though, a woven runner of flowers is effective and does not take up as much surface area.

Materials

Flowers and foliage

15 x stem's pink *Rosa* 'Aqua'
20 x stems pink stock (*Matthiola incana*)
about 20 stems *Eucalyptus gunnii* foliage
20 x pink *Centaurea*
10 x pink lisianthus (*Eustoma*)
10 x pink snap dragon (*Antirrhinum*)
10 x stems mint (*Mentha*)

Sundries

1 double plastic tray
2 x bricks wet foam
pot tape

Method

1. Soak the bricks of foam, then place in the shallow plastic tray (longer trays can be used for larger designs). Tape in the foam using the green pot tape. The wider pot tape is best as it gives extra security.

2. Place the foliage in a diamond shape on the outer edges of the foam. Ensure you place the stems – angled slightly downwards - near the rim of the container and not half way up the side of the foam.

   To achieve the diamond shape, the two shorter lengths should be approximately half the length of the two longer stems. Place only a few shorter stems into the centre at a 45° angle, but leave gaps for the flowers. Do not be tempted to cover the foam at this stage, or there will be little space to insert flower stems securely.

3. Place the focal roses so that they create a 'lazy S' running through the centre of the design. Stand the central rose vertically in the very centre of the foam – this should be the tallest point in the spray. Diagonally place two roses very close to it, one on either side, and angled slightly towards the outside of the design. This close proximity draws the eye to the centre.

4. Position some *Eustoma* flowers, with longer stems than the roses, towards the outer edges of the design. Place some slightly shorter ones towards the centre of the design on an angle as they reach the centre. The aim is to place transitional flowers in a diagonal grouping through the design. Place other transitional flowers in the opposite diagonal direction. Ensure you recess some of the transitional flowers, which creates a sense of movement and gives depth (see Glossary page 190).

5. Add the other flowers to complete the design. Angle the stems to give a flowing appearance.

6. Finally, tuck in additional foliage to fill any gaps.

Tips

- It is important to tape the foam securely because funeral designs are handled several times by funeral directors.
- Be mindful of the 23 cm (9 in) height restriction to ensure that no heads snap when in the hearse.
- If using lilies, buy them a week in advance for maximum impact. Pull out the pollen stamens, which will stain pallbearers' jackets.

Alternative flowers and foliage

Focal Flowers – Asiatic or Oriental lilies, sunflowers (*Helianthus*), *Allium*, large *Gerbera*, *Paeonia*.

Transitional flowers – Standard and spray *Dianthus*, *Alstroemeria*, *Phlox*, *Astilbe*, guelder rose (*Viburnum opulus*), tulips (long French tulips are excellent for cascading over the sides), *Trachelium*, larkspur, statice (*Limonium*), September flower (*Aster*).

Foliage – soft ruscus (*Danae racemosa*) - excellent for its soft arching habit and is readily available, ivy (*Hedera helix*) trails, *Photinia*, salal (*Gaultheria*), ladder fern (*Nephrolepis*).

2

4

Twig wreath

Use

This design is a natural, rustic-style tribute, which is suitable for a male colleague, friend or neighbour. The circular form of the wreath denotes eternity and it is an informal style.

As more people opt for alternative funeral services such as woodland burials – and there is generally a greater awareness of sustainability issues - there is an increasing demand for bio-degradable tributes. For these, it is imperative to use materials that rot and will not harm the environment. Alternative mediums to foam, for instance, could be moss, straw or twigs, which can be bound or attached using twine, rope, or even paper-covered binding wire.

The analogous colours orange, yellow and brown (as used in this illustration) suggest strength and masculinity, but the bereaved usually request specific colours or flowers that were favourites of the deceased. This design also creates a late winter/early spring look due to the seasonal materials used, including bare vines. The flowers are placed in plastic water phials disguised with brown stem tape.

Materials

Flowers and foliage

Vitis cognetiae vines
3 x stems orange amaryllis (*Hippeastrum*)
8 x yellow roses
10 x *Euphorbia fulgens*

Sundries

about 15 plastic water phials
brown stem tape
15 x 0.71 mm gauge stub wires
terracotta-coloured reindeer moss
naturally-skeletonised *Magnolia* leaves

1

3

Method

1. Use several vines to form a circle, by bending them over and under each other, which will help to secure them. Continue to do this with more vines until you have created a thick circular frame. If the vines do not stay in place, secure with short lengths of stub wire.

2. Cover the plastic phials with brown stem tape. This camouflages them against the brown vines. Cover some stub wires with brown tape and attach to the top of the phial just below the rim. Twist the wires together to secure. Fill the phials with water and replace the plastic lids. Secure the phials to the vine.

3. Cut off the rose and amaryllis heads so that the stems fit into the phials with their heads resting on top. Position these in clusters of about three heads all round the vine wreath. Distribute the groups of flowers evenly. You will need approximately three phials per grouping.

4. Defoliate the *Euphorbia* stems and add to the phials. If there is insufficient room in the phials attach the stems to the wreath using paper-covered wire.

5. Lightly spray the design with water and store in a cool place until required.

Tips

- Remove the *Euphorbia* leaves with scissors; pulling will snap its flowers.
- To stop the *Euphorbia* stems bleeding, place the ends in shallow water until it stops.
- If the *Euphorbia* is not being placed in water phials, it should be added to the design as close to delivery time as possible.
- The white sap exuded by *Euphorbia* can be a skin irritant, so wash hands thoroughly after handling.
- Save the water phials that are supplied with *Anthurium* and orchid flowers.

Alternative materials

Oriental lilies, sunflowers (*Helianthus*), calla lilies (*Zantedeschia*), *Craspedia*, china grass (*Liriope muscari*), *Typha*, *Oncidium* orchids, *Crocosmia*.

Personalised tributes

Use

Tributes that spell a loved one's name are a popular choice and are often seen placed upright against the side of the coffin inside the hearse, which makes them very visible as the cortege makes its way to the service.

Any name can be depicted in flowers but many are made up of letters such as MUM, DAD or NAN. The bases are made from florists' foam which can be purchased with a hard plastic base or a hard foam base. These individual letters clip onto a plastic stand which allows the tribute to be placed in an upright position, at a slight angle, giving best visibility.

The most effective basing material to use is white double *Chrysanthemum* as it gives the letters maximum clarity. Sometimes mixed flowers are used on each letter and whilst this can look pretty, the overall effect is not as clear as using the white double *Chrysanthemum*. Letters are edged either with foliage such as the single salal leaf (*Gaultheria shallon*) as shown here or pleated polypropylene ribbon.

With any name, it is usual to attach a spray of flowers at each end of the name. The sprays should be in diagonal opposite positions, one on the first letter and the other on the last letter. Generally, the spray of flowers needs to be quite small so that it does not hide the letter.

Materials

Flowers and foliage

4 x stems salal (*Gaultheria shallon*) per letter. These should be graded for size with some slightly smaller ones for the inside of the letters.

8 x stems white double *Chrysanthemum* per letter.

NB. This will vary with variety as some are 'fluffier' than others. In the winter months, flower heads can be slightly smaller.

Sundries

Letters as appropriate – illustrated here is the letter D

plastic stand on which to clip the letters

florists' scissors and knife

water mister

For spray (spray not shown here, refer to pages 106 - 108) –

small piece of foam to attach onto letter

pot tape to attach foam to letter

Tip

- Construct one letter at a time and grade the flower heads into different sizes. This makes the basing process much easier.

- It may take three or five rows of *Chrysanthemum* depending on the variety.

Alternative materials

Base

Autumn – *Hydrangea macrophylla* or *Sedum spectabile*.

Winter – carpet moss (*Plagiothecium undulatum*), bun moss (*Leucobryum glaucum*), smooth leaves such as cherry laurel (*Prunus laurocerasus*).

Summer – *Trachelium*, *Rosa*.

Spray flowers

Freesia, spray carnations (*Dianthus*), statice (*Limonium*).

Method

1. If you are using small pieces of foam for sprays (not shown) place these into position onto the first and last letter with either hot melt glue or pot tape - the latter is more secure. A 'Le Bump' could be used though this is more expensive and can be bulky. Ensure the foam pieces are placed diagonally opposite each other i.e. top left of first letter and bottom right of last letter or visa-versa.

2. Attach the letters to the plastic base and place under a tap to soak the foam. Do this for only a short time until the foam is soaked through. Do not leave under the water for any longer as it will become too heavy. The edge of the letters can then be slightly chamfered.

3. Create the edging first - either by inserting foliage (as illustrated) or pinning on a pleated length of ribbon. Single leaves sometimes need to be individually stitched (see page 40) in order to position them neatly. Alternatively, ensure the stem is clean before inserting into the foam as this will be more secure.

4. The edging leaves on the inside of the letters will need to be slightly smaller so as not to distort the shape of the letter. Once the edging is complete on all letters, begin the basing.

5. Cut the chrysanthemums leaving stems of approximately 5 cm (2 in). The chrysanthemums used on the top of the letters will need to be slightly longer than those on the outer edge. Grade the heads into small, medium and large.

a) First use the smaller heads. Place them securely into the inside of the letter, horizontally.

b) Place the medium heads in a single row next to the foliage - the base of the head should touch the foam to maintain the crispness and clarity of the outline.

c) Position the larger heads in the centre of these two outside rows to form a single central top row. This will define the shape of the letter. These should be placed vertically against the other chrysanthemums to form a neat uniform base coverage and to give a slightly rounded profile.

6. If you are using sprays on the letter construct in the same way as for the based wreath (see pages 106 - 108).

3

5

5

Sympathy wreath

Materials

Flowers and Foliage

5 x calla lily (*Zantedeschia*)
20 x purple *Anemone*
25 x *Rosa*
2½ x manzanita (*Arctostaphylos*) branches
3 x *Hydrangea*
10 x lisianthus (*Eustoma*)
1 bunch of *Ageratum*
1 bunch of *Asparagus setaceus* (asparagus fern)
1 bunch of *Asparagus densiflorus* 'Myersii' (foxtail fern)
1 bunch of *Polystichum munitum* (sword fern)
8 x bunches *Galax*
1 bunch *Eucalyptus*
1 plant/cut *Kalanchoe* 'Magic Bells'
1 bunch of *Eryngium*

Sundries

metal wreath stand available from arts and crafts stores in the US
55 cm (22 in) wreath frame

Use

This style of funeral wreath is commonly used in the United States of America. The wreath is placed upright on a stand besides the coffin, which enables it to be seen easily.

Funeral tributes in the USA reflect the sender's emotions rather than tradition. The US is a melting pot of many cultures, so there are no universal customs or typical tributes. Instead, seasonality is key.

The designer considers any specific sentiments of the sender and reflects this with appropriate flowers and foliage. A winter funeral, for instance, uses evergreens, bark, and pine cones; while a spring service incorporates bulb flowers, blossom and emerging foliage.

Colour is important, too: some senders choose a vibrant tribute, but others prefer a muted palette to reflect a more sombre feeling.

Method

1. Soak the foam in water by placing it in a large sink. If you do not have one that is large enough, you may need to hold the wreath under a tap and move it around like a steering wheel.

2. Cover the metal stand with branches or foliage of your choice. This design uses manzanita branches, foxtail and asparagus ferns. Hang the wreath on the stand and cover lightly with foliage. Here, the wreath was covered with small lengths of the foxtail and asparagus ferns.

3. Create a focal area at the top of the design with the calla lilies, lisianthus, *Ageratum*, *Hydrangea* and 'Magic Bells'.

4. Place the remaining flowers and foliage through the wreath to cover. At Winston's (where this wreath was designed) we use three techniques to mimic the way that flowers and foliage present themselves in nature. 'veiling', a term used to denote partially obscuring or softening the appearance of a stronger flower by placing a delicate piece of foliage such as asparagus fern to partially cover or 'veil'. We also use 'shadowing', which denotes the use of two flowers of the same variety, one behind the other to create a shadow effect. The third technique is grouping, which describes the placing of multiple flowers of the same variety in varied sizes of clusters to create focal points. These three techniques have been used in this design.

Tips

- Employ simple, natural designs and monochrome colour palettes to create a feeling of calm, peace and serenity.

- Foliage makes the difference. Maintain a balance of textures, sizes and shades. Place hard glossy leaves next to softer textured foliage for contrast.

Alternative flowers

Helianthus, Paeonia, Trachelium, Scabious, Hydrangea, Godetia, Gerbera, Dahlia.
This wreath is large and uses lots of stems. To create a smaller version, simply reduce proportionally the number of stems of each flower and foliage.

2

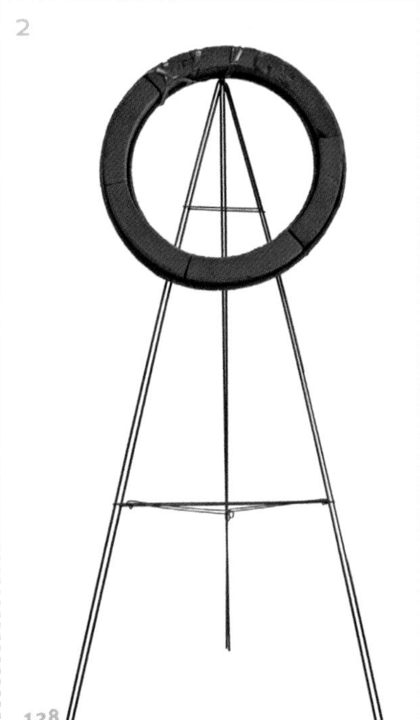

2

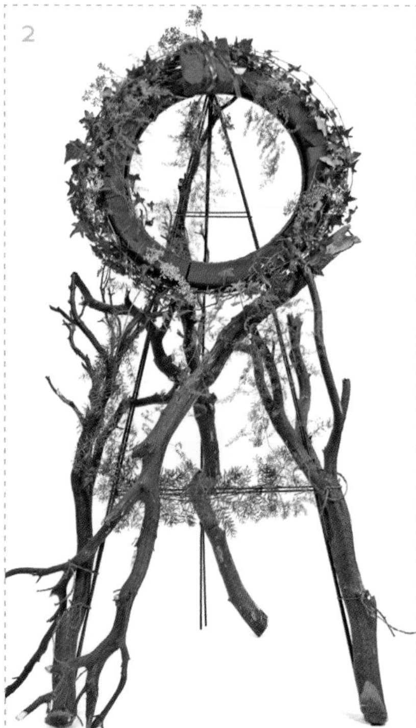

4

chapter 8

Contract work

Contract flowers can form an important part of a florist's work. Whatever the highs and lows of the retail year, they are a welcome weekly order. However, the florist needs to be innovative in order to retain such work - and there are many other factors to consider.

Longevity is important. The materials need to look good for the week's duration - this does, however, need to be balanced with materials that are not too long lasting. If, for example, exotics such as *Anthurium*, *Strelitzia* or orchids are used, the client may wish to retain them for two weeks resulting in lost business. In such instances, a combination could be considered, so that even if some materials are still looking good, others may not thus ensuring that the whole design still needs to be changed.

Contract designs are not always well-maintained and must therefore be able to survive on a minimum amount of moisture, or placed into water directly. This is why tied designs in vases are often used for contracts: the flowers will last better than they would in foam, which will dry out quickly in a warm office. This does not exclude the use of foam, though, as exotic materials anchored in it will last quite happily in a warm environment.

The use of seasonal materials will help to keep the designs constantly changing and topical, but be cautious about soft spring flowers unless kept directly in water and in a cool environment. Alternative longer-lasting flowers could be amaryllis (*Hippeastrum*). Twigs could be a winter alternative, whilst the soft, summery herbaceous flowers such as *Scabiosa, Eremurus, Eryngium* are summer options. Autumn brings *Sedum, Crocosmia, Dahlia, Rudbeckia* and berries. Be cautious with berries, though, as *Hypericum* is the only one which will not become soft and soggy with age - it is therefore the most viable to use.

Broad leaves give impact and last, but to improve their surface texture give them a spray of leaf shine.

Sometimes simply varying the containers helps to give variety, but remember they should be sufficiently tall to support the flowers and be stable.

Coffee table arrangement

Use

For placement on a low, occasional table where the design is generally viewed from above and where space may be limited.

There is an implication that there should be enough space for coffee cups and perhaps the odd newspaper, so the design should not take up too much surface area.

This design is a classic round arrangement enhanced by the natural earthy container and the use of looped bear grass to create space on the outer edges. The bowl itself does not take up too much space, though the circumference of the flowers make the design seem slightly larger than it actually is – and therefore good value for money.

Classic white and green always work together, particularly with the natural pale stone of the bowl in the illustration.

Materials

Flowers and foliage

10 x white roses
15 x white *Bouvardia*
5 x white *Phlox*
7 x ivy (*Hedera helix*) trails
2 x ming fern (*Asparagus densiflorus* 'Mysersii')
4 x strands bear grass (*Xerophyllum tenax*)
Sphagnum moss (optional)

Sundries

round container
1 brick of wet florists' foam
Cellophane to line the container (if porous)
0.46 mm gauge silver wire (to wire the tips of the bear grass)

Method

1. Line the container with Cellophane or plastic (if porous). Soak the foam for one minute and place into the container. Pack the foam securely with either the smaller off-cuts of foam, or with a little sphagnum moss. Ensure there is sufficient room for watering.

2. Cut the ming fern into lengths of approximately 20 cm (8 in) and defoliate about the last 5 cm (2 in) from the stem end. Ming fern is used mainly as a filler to hide the foam rather than an outline shape. Cut the ivy trails into slightly longer lengths of approximately 25 cm (10 in). Place the foliage in a circular effect around the edge of the foam, angling them down slightly over the container. Intersperse the ming fern and the ivy.

3. Do not add foliage to the top of the foam. Leave it empty so that you can position the flowers with ease. Place the top, central rose first: this will act as a guide for the other roses. It should stand slightly taller than the rest of the plant material and should be about two thirds of the height of the container; in this case approximately 20 cm (8 in), which allows for part of the stem to be inserted into the foam.

4. To emphasise the focal rose, place two roses slightly lower either side. Place two further roses on the outer edges of the design to give a central curved line. These other blooms should be inserted at a 45° angle to create the impression that the stems are radiating from a central point.

5. Once a focal line has been established, distribute the rest of the plant materials throughout the circular outline. Using diagonal groupings in a small-scale posy design can give a blocked look and it is often more pleasing to simply distribute materials evenly.

6. Recess some materials at a lower level to avoid monotony and keep the eye moving throughout the arrangement.

7. Fill in any gaps in the foam with foliage. Do not over fill with spare flowers, because the design will look too full. Every flower should be surrounded by a small amount of space.

8. Insert two stem ends of bear grass at different levels on one side and then mount wire the ends with fine silver wire (see page 34). Insert the mounted ends into the foam at another point allowing the grass to curve over the flowers without touching them. Do the same on the other side. This enhances the design by using a contrasting form and creating more space.

9. Lightly spray the design with water.

Tips

Rounded flowers help to reinforce the round shape of a posy arrangement. A filler foliage is essential to cover the foam in this design.

Symmetrical triangle design

Use

This traditional British triangular design is symmetrical in shape. It is front facing and ideal for contract work - perhaps for a company's reception where it would be viewed primarily from the front.

Although front facing, it is essential to position materials so that the eye is led round to the back of the design to give depth and interest. In floristry training it is one of the first designs to be mastered as it forms a basis from which other design principles can be applied. It is effectively the same design as a pedestal arrangement on a smaller scale.

A range of containers can be used – from plastic dishes to more elaborate ceramic containers. There should always be sufficient depth of foam to allow the stems to be angled over the container to achieve the required width and depth. Containers that are slightly elevated tend to add height and allow cascading materials to be used at the front and sides giving more elegance.

Materials

Flowers and foliage

7 x soft ruscus (*Danae racemosa*)
5 x red mini *Gerbera*
8 x spray carnation (*Dianthus*)
6 x red *Alstroemeria*
4 x *Leucadendron* 'Safari Sunset'

Sundries

½ brick florists' foam
green plastic container
pot tape
florists' knife and scissors

Method

1. Soak the foam and cut to fit inside the container, allowing sufficient depth of foam above the container. Lightly chamfer the edges of the top of the foam.

2. Secure the foam in the container with pot tape.

3. Establish the outline shape using the ruscus. Aim for a triangular shape. The tallest piece of ruscus should be placed at the back to establish the height. There should be two shorter pieces placed on each side resting on the rim of the container to establish the width and a further piece at the front for the depth.

4. Fill in with more foliage. Ensure there is not too much height at the top to avoid a 'fan' shape. Remember to defoliate the lower stems by about 8 cm (3 in) to make insertion into the foam more secure.

5. Once the outline of the foliage is complete place the five central flowers (the mini *Gerbera*) in a 'lazy S' pattern. The central flower should be three quarters of the way down from the top foliage and be placed at an angle. It should be the most prominent flower.

6. Place two more mini *Gerbera* diagonally opposite and at a lower level. The remaining two should be positioned on the outer edges - the top one in line with the focal flower and the lower one diagonally opposite the third flower. The overall pattern should resemble a 'lazy S' shape.

7. Position the less impactive 'transitional' flowers. Place the red spray carnations in a diagonal grouping. This means that if you placed them at the top left of the focal flowers they should sweep halfway down that side and stop level with the focal flower. They should then be continued down on the opposite lower right side. Similarly with the *Alstroemeria*. Place these first top right and then curved through to the bottom left. All materials except for the top vertical ones should be placed at angles to achieve a flowing, radiating appearance.

8. Fill in the gaps with the other plant material such as the *Leucadendron*. Their deep red colour will give visual depth at the centre. Remember there should be flowers on different levels so some recession (positioning on a lower level) should be evident.

Tip

There is nothing wrong in simply distributing the transitional flowers evenly through the design but if there is a limited amount of a flower or foliage then diagonal groupings are the best way to maximise visual impact.

Vegetative within a square

Use

This style of design is suitable for a hotel reception, or similar venue - such as an upmarket office reception where an initial impact is paramount.

The vegetative style (see page 191) is naturalistic and requires plant materials to be used sympathetically with respect to their growth pattern.

This version is made in a shallow square container, which emphasises the height of the lovely green *Viburnum opulus* 'Roseum'.

A note of caution, however: the shallow depth of these vegetative designs makes transportation challenging and therefore they are often better created on site. Always choose materials for contract designs that will look good for one week. *Viburnum* for instance, can be temperamental which is why the illustrated design has been constructed on pinholders rather than floral foam in order to allow the direct uptake of water.

Materials

Flowers and foliage

5 x guelder rose (*Viburnum opulus* 'Roseum')
6 x tulips
3 x hyacinths (*Hyacinthus*)
reindeer moss (*Cladonia rangiferina*) for base

Sundries

15 cm^2 (6 in^2) shallow square container
4 x pin holders approximately 6 cm (2 ½ in) in diameter
3 x thin garden canes

Method

1. Put the pin holders in the container and fill with water. There is no need to adhere fixative on the base as the lead weight of the pinholders holds them securely. This design is not transportable – you need to make it in situ.

2. Insert the tallest stem of *Viburnum* by placing it firmly onto the metal spikes in the pinholders. Evenly distribute the other stems around the container. Add the tulips which will naturally be shorter in length. Distribute these evenly around the container.

3. Prepare the hyacinths by inserting a thin garden cane up into the centre of the stem. Place this onto the pinholder. They will naturally sit lower and provide a pleasing contrast of colour and height.

4. Finally, add some reindeer moss to the base to cover the pinholders.

Alternative materials

These upright designs need some materials that naturally stand straight with some shorter underplanting types at the base. Flat saucer-like flowers such as Gerbera do not work well in this type of design.

For height – dogwood (*Cornus*), lisianthus (Eustoma), roses, *Liatris, Aconitum, Antirrhinum, Kniphofia, Anigozanthus, Crocosmia, Sandersonia, Prunus triloba.*

For underplanting – *Muscari, Triteleia, Centaurea, Fritillaria.*

2

Tip

Place the central components first for ease and to minimise damage of outer materials.

Modern arrangement using *Allium* blooms

Use

This would make an ideal contract arrangement for the reception desk of a smart office or hotel. The decorative onions (*Allium*) and foliage will remain fresh-looking for one week.

It is a simple, linear arrangement and illustrates the importance of space when creating modern designs. The bold round forms of the *Allium* are allowed to steal the show supported by the restful green *Helleborus* at the base, and *Iris* leaves for height. The crossing and quirkiness of the twiggy *Corokia* serves to bring some contrasting lightness of form against the bolder components. The grey pewter-like container is a good colour link with the purple *Allium* without competing in any way.

Allium is a genus of the onion family (*Alliaceae*) and therefore has a slight smell of onion.

Materials

Flowers and foliage

4 x purple *Allium* 'Gladiator'
3 x *Helleborus* leaves
2 x *Iris* leaves
1 branch *Corokia cotoneaster*
carpet moss to cover foam

Sundries

vase – this one is 30 cm (12 in) tall
wet foam sufficient (to fill container)
Cellophane (to line container)
0.71 mm gauge green stub wires (to make pins)
florists' knife and scissors

Method

1. Soak the foam and line the container. Metal containers like the one illustrated may leak through the side seams so always line to be certain.
2. Ensure the foam sits just level with, or slightly below, the container.
3. Place the *Allium* flowers in a vertical, staggered line by first positioning the tallest to the centre back and then position successive blooms slightly to one side of each other.
4. Next position the *Corokia* stem to the side, opposite the lowest flower. Place the two Iris stems together on the opposite side, behind the *Allium* blooms. These will insert more easily into the foam if you cut the stem end on the diagonal.
5. Place the *Helleborus* leaves in a close grouping at the base to give visual depth. Hide any exposed foam by pinning on the carpet moss.

Tip

Choose strong architectural forms to give impact. Large leaves at the base will give visual depth as well as hide the foam. Ensure there are no more than five different materials to maintain a contemporary look.

4

Alternative materials

Flowers – sunflowers (*Helianthus*), *Strelitzia*, king protea (*P. cynaroides*).
Twigs – twisted hazel (*Corylus avellana* 'Contorta'), twisted willow (*Salix babylonica var. pekinensis* 'Tortuosa').
Foliage – *Fatsia japonica*, *Philodendron scandens* or *Philodendron* 'Xanadu'.

Spring arrangement with a structure

Use

This contemporary design would suit a low table in a reception area.

The base twigs of winter and early spring lend themselves for manipulation into structures and frameworks, which make a lovely decorative medium through which plant materials can be woven.

These structures are easy to make if there is sap in the twigs, so they are best kept in water once cut and not allowed to dry out and go brittle.

Twigs such as hazel (*Corylus*), dogwood (*Cornus*) and willow (*Salix*) are ideal for straight angular structures, whilst bendy vines, such as Vitis cognetiae, are ideal for round or curved frameworks such as for the rim of a round or oval container.

Water phials can be attached to these structures, which is better for spring flowers that do not last long in foam.

Brown paper-covered bind wire is ideal for attaching twigs together as it adheres around the twigs better than bare wire and has more strength than twine.

If foam is being used in a container, it should be no higher than the level of the container, or even slightly lower. An attractive surface dressing, such as moss or pebbles, can be added to cover the foam.

Materials

Flowers and foliage

lengths of birch (*Betula pentula*)
dogwood (*Cornus*)
20 x tulips (*Tulipa*)
10 x stems *Craspedia*

Sundries

1½ bricks of foam
oval container
moss or pebbles (to cover foam)
0.90 mm gauge stub wire
tubes/phials

Tips

If you are using plastic phials, they need to be filled with water first and then replace their lids. Glass ones can be filled after being placed on the structure using a pipette.

Alternative materials

Materials need to have a degree of flexibility to work in this design.

Calla lilies (*Zantedeschia*), *Craspedia*, *Oncidium* 'Golden Showers' orchids.

Method

1. Soak the foam (see page 191). Place it into the container and cut it level (or just below if pebbles are being placed on the foam).

2. Cover the top of the foam with pebbles and moss (use wire hairpins to attach moss).

3. Prepare the framework by creating three circles with the dogwood (*Cornus*) stems (one slightly larger than the other two), and secure each one with paper-covered wire.

4. Take a long length of the dogwood and attach it to all three circles, place them in a line and spaced out from each other (no longer than the container they will sit on).

   Continue to add lengths of birch until you have created a suitable structure.

5. Attach this to the foam by using long hairpins. Ensure it is attached all the way around.

6. Attach glass or plastic water phials to the framework using the paper-covered bind wire. Intersperse them with space between to get an even distribution of the tulips.

7. Cut the tulips to the required length and place them in the water phials. Ensure the stems are sufficiently long, because they are a feature of this design as much as the heads. Tuck in the stems of *Craspedia*. These will survive well out of water.

4

7

Modern winter handtied

Use

Handtied designs are ideal for contract work, because they can be placed directly in water and the flower materials will last as long as possible. They provide many opportunities to be creative with vases - by placing coloured nuggets in the water of a clear glass vase, or wrapping the vase with a broad leaf such as *Aspidistra* to change the look.

In fact, clear glass vases are very versatile. They can instantly convey a theme when filled with different items: colourful sweets for a children's party; sliced citrus fruits for summer; or Mikado sticks for a Japanese restaurant. When using glass, ensure it is scrupulously clean and without chips.

Care should be given to cover the binding points of handtieds in clear vases (if the stems are to be seen). You could wrap the stems with a plain broad leaf such as *Aspidistra* and bind with a decorative wire.

The bold, modern handtied in the illustration creates impact through the grouping of amaryllis (*Hippeastrum*) at the base of the design. The design has a wintry look, and the rich reds make it ideal for a reception desk in November and December.

The natural curve of the *Euphorbia fulgens* on the left side gives the design width; materials with a natural curve help to avoid any side placements looking too rigid and horizontal.

Most limited handtieds benefit from a collar of foliage at the base, which has a dual purpose: it gives this design visual depth while providing balance to prevent the handtied falling forward. In this example, aralia (*Fatsia japonica*) has been used.

The kangaroo paw (*Anigozanthus*) at the top gives height and a contrast of form. It also lasts very well in warm conditions making it ideal for use in contract work.

Materials

Flowers and foliage

3 x red amaryllis (*Hippeastrum*)
3 x red kangaroo paw (*Anigozanthus*)
3 x aralia (*Fatsia japonica*) leaves
7 x *Euphorbia fulgens*
2 x standard red carnations
2 x small kentia palm (*Howea forsteriana*)
1 *Aspidistra* leaf

Sundries

about 1 m (3½ ft) of twine, or paper-covered wire (to tie)
medium-height glass tank
decorative pebbles for base (optional)

Tip

- If the tied design will not stand upright, attach a grid of clear adhesive tape around the rim of the container, thereby narrowing the opening. This should help to make it secure. Placing decorative nuggets at the base would also help. If used, ensure they are washed well beforehand to avoid any dirt particles floating in the water.
- Take care of the *Euphorbia* sap, which is an irritant.

Alternative materials

Bold flowers – *Allium*, sunflowers, *Heliconia*, *Banksia*.
Transitional Flowers – *Lecadendron*, *Grevillea*, *Nerine*, *Sandersonia*.

Method

1. Defoliate the *Euphorbia*. In contemporary designs it looks neater without leaves. Neither the amaryllis nor the kangaroo paw have leaves, though the lower branches of the latter will need removing so the stem is bare approximately two thirds of the way up.

2. Support wire the three *Fatsia* leaves by stitching each using a long 0.71 mm gauge green-coated wire (see page 34). The lower leaflets of the kentia palms will also need removing to make the palm a little smaller.

3. Once you have defoliated all the materials, they are ready to put together. Select an appropriately sized glass vase and fill it with clean water. Have the tying material ready, too.

4. Take the tallest stem of kangaroo paw and add the other two at slightly lower levels.

5. Follow the same method as that of the tied sheaf and any front facing handtied. The first central materials will be very straight, but thereafter, place any materials to the left on top of each other, and place any to the right behind the ones before. The stems will spiral, not cross.

6. After the kangaroo paw, add the two amaryllis in staggering heights with the most open at the base just above the tie point. All the stems will be more or less parallel at this stage.

2

7. Next take two or three of the *Euphorbia* stems and add to the left side with the stems going on a diagonal angle on top of the other stems. Add the remaining *Euphorbia* to this group, but at a slightly shorter length so the group is staggered. Place the stems on top of the ones before.

8. Add the two palms, again one slightly shorter than the other, on to the right side. The stems should be tucked behind the ones before.

9. Finally, add the two or three *Fatsia* leaves to the front under the lower amaryllis, bending them at a right angle so they will curve slightly over the rim of the vase. Secure all the materials together with a length of twine, ribbon or paper-covered bind wire. Wrap a long piece around the stems several times and pull securely with each bind. To finish the binding point, cut out the hard stalk of the *Aspidistra* leaf and wrap it around. Secure this with a little red wire and place the design in the vase.

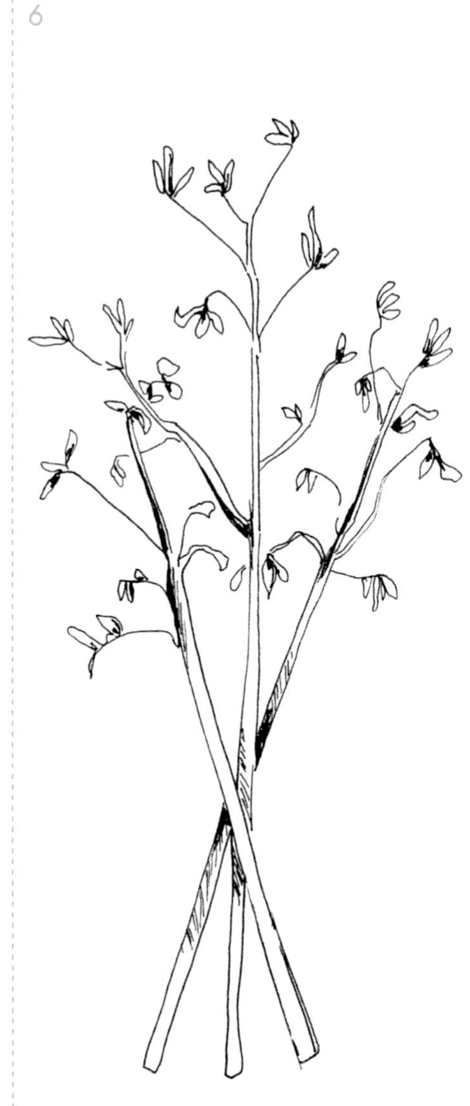

6

ГОСТ 1770-74
1000МЛ
2 КЛ 20°C Н

chapter 9

Weddings, parties and functions

Flowers help us to celebrate many special occasions in life, including weddings, christenings, birthdays and anniversaries. These special events provide us with an opportunity to be adventurous and – budget permitting – extravagant with flowers.

Such occasions sometimes provide a theme or significant colour scheme to work to, which will determine the choice of design and flower materials used.

At Christmas and Easter, flowers can be used to dress the home or a venue. Christmas is often associated with the decoration of fir trees (hailing from Victorian times) and garlands, which deck stairs and mantelpieces. Evergreen foliage has long been evident in winter decorating, and is a symbol of survival. As well as green, rich reds, wintery white and silver are often used.

Easter heralds the start of spring, when plants burst into life, and we decorate with bright yellows, pinks and lime greens to mirror the season.

Other popular traditions include Mothering Sunday, Valentine's Day and Halloween (which is becoming popular in the UK).

Personal celebrations may include exam successes, moving home, getting engaged, or simply a thank-you gesture.

Other nationalities and religions have their own celebrations. For the Chinese, New Year is a significant occasion, and they decorate with orange trees and blossom. For Jewish New Year celebrations, potted plant arrangements are often incorporated.

Some religions use four-posted canopy structures as a setting for their marriage ceremonies; the Jewish have the chuppah, and Hindus, the mandap. Large garlands are ideal to swag around the poles of these structures, and smaller, more delicate garlands adorn the bridal couple.

Pedestal arrangement

Use

Pedestal arrangements are ideal for churches, hotels and marquees. By definition, these designs are raised on a plinth or stand to give height. They are usually symmetrical, and although many designs are front-facing (viewed primarily from the front and placed against a wall), they can also be created for all-round viewing.

Sometimes the container to be used will be a plastic bowl which is completely hidden. However, on other occasions, an urn is visible and an integral part of the design. The container should always be large enough to support the weight of the stems.

Bowls should contain at least two standard bricks of foam, or even better - a solid larger block of OASIS® Jumbo foam or pedestal bricks. Urns, however, are often better with scrunched chicken wire and water – particularly if temperamental flowers are being used such as lilac (*Syringa vulgaris*), or guelder rose (*Viburnum opulus*), because these flowers benefit from having their stem ends directly in water. They will need to have very tall stems, to achieve the correct proportions - otherwise foam and extension cones will need to be used. Where very long, heavy materials are used, it is advisable to cover the foam with a piece of large chicken wire to help keep it intact.

The plinth on which the arrangement stands should be both secure and appropriate to the setting, as this will always be visible. It is also important to consider the surface on which it will be standing. For instance, if placed on an uneven covered lawn in a marquee, the base must be strong and stable with a greater surface area.

Traditional black metal stands are often telescopic, which is useful for transporting since they can be reduced in size. However, they are not as safe for large, heavy designs and not secure on an uneven surface. Wooden plinths are effective as they withstand weight, look aesthetically pleasing and can be painted different colours if required.

The pedestal design, like all large-scale designs, is easier to create at the venue rather than being transported.

Materials

Flowers and foliage

20 x stems soft ruscus (*Danae racemosa*)
10 x smoke bush (*Cotinus*)
5 x large peony (*Paeonia*)
10 x large *Delphinium*
20 x purple larkspur (*Delphinium consolida*)
20 x pink lisianthus (*Eustoma russellianum*)
20 x guelder rose (*Viburnum opulus*)
10 x pink single *Chrysanthemum*

Sundries

large green plastic bowl
2 x standard bricks of floral foam or a block of OASIS® 'Jumbo' foam or an OASIS® pedestal brick
pot tape (wide)
plinth

Tips

- To achieve more height with short-stemmed flowers like peonies, tape a plastic extension cone to a piece of bamboo, fill with water and insert the flower or foliage.
- For a more modern appearance, group bold materials such as *Allium giganteum* with other compatible materials, such as *Gerbera*, and use tropical foliage such as yellow cane palm (*Dypsis*), phoenix palm (*Howea*) and *Monstera* leaves.
- Choice stems such as *Phalaenopsis* orchids will be lost, as will small-headed flowers. Pedestals are the ideal designs for inexpensive chrysanthemums, so volume can be obtained.

Method

1. Soak the foam. Place in an upright position in the container to ensure there is a generous amount of foam extending above the rim. This is essential, as stems will need to be angled over the sides.

2. Secure the foam in the container using pot tape. Tape over several times to ensure security.

3. Establish the outline shape using soft ruscus and aim for a triangular shape. Place the tallest stem of soft ruscus at the back to establish the height. Place two shorter pieces each side resting on the rim of the container to establish the width, then place a piece at the front for depth. Once these basic dimensions are in place, this outline should be filled in with the other foliage. Any other foliage can be added – such as the *Cotinus* used here – in a diagonal grouping from one side through to its diagonal opposite. This is visually pleasing and helps to achieve visual balance.

4. Ensure that there is not too much height to avoid a fan shape. Remember to defoliate the lower stems by about 8 cm (3 in) to make insertion into foam more secure.

5. Once the outline of foliage is complete, place the five central focal flowers (the peonies) in a 'lazy S' pattern. The central flower should be three quarters of the way down from the top foliage – it should be the most prominent flower.

6. Place two more focal flowers diagonally opposite and at a lower level. The remaining two should be positioned on the outer edges – the top one in line with the focal flower and the lower one diagonally opposite the third flower. The overall pattern should resemble a 'lazy S.'

7. Add the less impactful, transitional flowers. Place the pink lisianthus (*Eustoma*) in a diagonal grouping. This means that if you place them to the top left of the focal flowers, they should sweep halfway down that side and stop level with the focal flower. Then continue down on the opposite, lower right side. Place the guelder rose in a similar manner; insert them top right first and curve through to the bottom left. There is nothing wrong in simply distributing the transitional flowers evenly through the design, but if there is a limited amount of a flower or foliage, diagonal groupings are the best way to maximise the visual impact.

8. All materials (apart from the top vertical ones) should be placed at angles to achieve a flowing, radiating appearance.

9. Take any flowers with less impact, such as the larkspur, through the design in similar groupings. Fill any obvious gaps with foliage rather than flowers. Remember there should be flowers on different levels so that some recession (positioning deeper in the design) is evident.

3

7

9

Classic posy arrangement

Use

The classic posy arrangement could form the basis for a table centre at any occasion. It is ideally suited to the round dinner tables that are often found in hotels and marquees, because it can be viewed from any angle and allows the occupants to see each other across the table.

This relatively simple, round arrangement has become a classic design, which can be modified and elaborated. It can be large or small according to the size of the table and can be adapted to include a candle. In this design, seasonal peonies (*Paeonia*) and *Astilbe* have been used, which convey a summer theme.

Materials

Flowers and foliage

7 – 9 x pink *Paeonia*
conifer (*Sequoia sempervirens* 'Adpressa')
7 x stems *Eucalyptus gunnii* foliage
8 x stems sweet William (*Dianthus barbatus*)
8 x stems blue larkspur
5 x stems double pink lisianthus (*Eustoma*)
10 x stems pink sweet pea (*Lathyrus odorathus*)

Sundries

1/3 brick florists' foam (wet)
shallow green plastic bowl
pot tape (narrow width preferably)
florists' scissors and knife

4

6

Method

1. Cut a standard brick of foam in half and soak.

2. Place the foam into the shallow plastic container and secure with pot tape, pulling securely over the foam and to the sides of the container.

3. Cut equal lengths of the *Eucalyptus* foliage to about 25 cm (10 in) long to allow for some stem to be inserted into the foam. Place in a circular shape around the edge of the foam at an equal distance from one another. All foliage should rest on the edge of the container at this point.

4. Add the peonies, which are the focal flowers. The central flower should be completely vertical and also slightly taller than the rest, which should be judged against the overall circumference of the design. This means that the wider the outline shape, the taller the central flower from which everything else should flow.

5. Immediately either side of the central flower, place two more flowers lower down, each at slightly different levels.

6. Place two slightly longer outer flowers to create a 'lazy S' pattern.

7. If you have more focal flowers, use them either side of this 'lazy S', to give even distribution. If you do not have more, place smaller transitional flowers within the circular outline. Begin with the outer edge of the arrangement and use slightly longer flowers. Use less open flowers towards the outer edge to achieve good size graduation.

8. Place the remaining flowers so that they all appear to radiate from the centre of the foam.

9. Fill in the gaps with more foliage, remembering that there should be space around each flower. If any flowers are overcrowded the design will look too compact and solid. Place flowers at slightly different levels for interest; blooms on slightly lower levels will force the eye into the design.

10. Spray lightly with water and keep away from direct sunlight and radiators.

Tips

- When you have finished, place the design on a table and look at it very carefully whilst sitting down, and you will notice any gaps.
- This arrangement can be easily adapted by replacing the central focal flower with a candle for an evening function.

Christmas table arrangement

Use

Table arrangements are widely used to grace the centre of a dinner table for a range of occasions. This design would particularly suit a long oval or rectangular table at Christmas time, as it uses rich red flowers and evergreen foliage complemented by a candle.

In fact, the use of contrasting foliage and berries at this time of year cuts down the necessity for flowers since other items, such as cones and lotus heads, can be used as an alternative. These dried materials can also be sprayed in any of the metallic colours to give a sense of Christmas sparkle, or simply left natural.

They are easy to assemble and if kept sprayed and away from a heat source can last for up to two weeks – particularly if carnations are used instead of roses.

Materials

Flowers and foliage

7 x *Rosa* 'Grand Prix' (fewer can be used if cones or lotus seed heads are also incorporated into the design)
7 x stems *Photinia* x *fraseri* 'Red Robin'
5 x stems *Pinus sylvestris*
7 x stems *Skimmia japonica*
5 x stems *Abies nobilis*
5 x stems *Cedrus atlantica*
2 x sprays guilded oak (*Quercus*)

Sundries

1 black plastic tray
1 brick of florists' foam (wet)
pot tape
scissors and secateurs
candle
candle cup or 0.90 mm gauge stub wires

Method

1. Soak the foam.

2. Place into the tray and secure with the pot tape, but take two strips either side of the centre of the foam in order to leave space for the candle.

3. If no candle cup is available, secure the candle in the foam by making four wire hairpins from the 0.90 mm stub wires leaving approximately 7 cm (3 in) in length. Tape these onto the end of the candle using the pot tape. The candle can then be placed on top of the foam in the centre and used as a focal point.

4. De-foliate the ends of the foliage so that a clean stem can be inserted more securely into the foam. Two longer pieces of approximately 20 - 25 cm (8 - 10 in) will be needed for the two longer sides of the arrangement.

5. Begin the outline of the arrangement by inserting the two longer outer pieces of foliage (in this example the long *Cedrus* foliage was used) to establish the length. These need to be placed on the end of the foam and pushed slightly up into it so they can be angled down over the edge of the container.

6. Then place two shorter pieces of cedar into the sides of the foam in line with the candle. Again, slightly angle the foliage down over the sides of the container to achieve a good flow of materials. This should give a simple, diamond shape in which to work. Other foliage should now be placed in between these four pieces at slightly shorter lengths to maintain a diamond shape. Once this outline has been achieved, shorter materials need to be placed into the centre of the foam – angled slightly to give the appearance of radiating out from the centre.

7. The main focal flowers (in this example roses are used, but carnations could be a substitute) should be placed in a 'lazy S' pattern through the centre and either side of the candle. They should be about 12 cm (5 in) in length.

8. Once the focal line of flowers has been placed, additional materials may be added such as cones, lotus heads or, for a shinier look, baubles work very well. These can be inserted by means of a medium gauge wire being threaded through the small wire loop at the top, with the ends of the wire twisted together and used as a prong to insert into the foam.

9. Finally fill any visible gaps by using any remaining foliage.

4

6

Tips

Fresh fruits such as apples and sliced pomegranates can also be used in the area below the candle.

Alternative Materials

Foliage – box (*Buxus sempevirens*), strawberry tree (*Arbutus unedo*), conifer (*Cupressus*), *Viburnum tinus*.
Flowers – standard *Dianthus*.

7

Winter twig arrangement

Use

This horizontal design would be ideal for a long table at any winter celebration, including Christmas.

It uses a minimal amount of flower materials – just amaryllis (*Hippeastrum*), calla lilies (*Zantedeschia*) and lichen-covered cedar (*Cedrus*) branches.

Both the amaryllis and callas are relatively long lasting, so this could also be a viable contract arrangement for the Christmas period. The rough-hewn texture of the bowl contrasts well with the white flowers and is sympathetic to the lichen-covered twigs.

Materials

Flowers and foliage

2 x amaryllis (*Hippeastrum*)
8 x calla lily (*Zantedeschia*)
8 x larch (*Larix decidua*) branches

Sundries

textured bowl
1 brick of florists' foam (wet)
Cellophane (to line container)
0.90 mm gauge wires or cocktail sticks (to support amaryllis)
0.71 mm gauge wires (to support callas)

Method

1. Soak the foam for approximately one minute until the air bubbles cease. Cut a piece of Cellophane or plastic and line the inside of the bowl (to avoid water seepage from the foam).

2. Cut the foam to fit the container, ensuring that there is approximately 5 cm (2 in) standing above the container – this will enable you to angle some materials over the side.

3. Cut the amaryllis short, leaving a small amount of stem, because you will need to place them low into the centre of the design. For ease of placing in the foam, insert a 0.90 mm gauge wire or cocktail stick up the centre of the stem. Do the same with the callas using the 0.71mm gauge wires. It will not be possible to insert the wire too far up the stem, but a support wire on the end will help (see page 34). Ensure a little of the wire is protruding from the end as this will act as a prong.

4. Begin by placing the twigs at either end of the foam. One side should have approximately four or five longer twigs than the other. It is best to place these first, so that the fragile head of the amaryllis is not damaged. Place the callas between the twigs; leave two slightly longer to give a staggered effect.

5. Place several flower heads from one amaryllis into a group in the centre – there should be one or two open heads and several smaller buds.

6. Take one or two callas and loop their stems over the central amaryllis head, which will create an enclosed space and draw attention to the dominant central area.

7. Fill in any gaps in the foam with some short filler foliage, such as ming fern (*Asparagus umbellatus*), or medium size leaves such as *Galax*, or ivy (*Hedera*). Mist the design lightly.

Tip

The amaryllis flower heads can be placed into a plastic water phial, which can then be inserted into the foam. This will extend their life a little longer than if placed directly in foam.

Alternative material

Flowers – *Lilium* 'Casa Blanca', *Nerine*, Arabian chincherinchee (*Ornithogalum arabicum*).
Twigs – willow (*Salix*), hazel (*Corylus avellana*).

S-shaped/circular table design

Use

Table arrangements are a perfect decoration for so many occasions where food is present.

This wintery white table centre, designed with Christmas in mind, includes small baubles and candles. It would be ideal for a long table, as it can snake through the centre.

The circular version is ideal for a round table and the S-shaped for a long, rectangular table. The technique for the two designs is the same. To create the mechanics for the S-shaped design cut the wreath ring into two equal semi-circles and glue together with hot glue to form an undulating shape.

Flowers and foliage

9 x Arabian chincherinchees (*Ornithogalum arabicum*)
blue spruce (*Abies procera*)
Scots pine (*Pinus sylvestris*)
blue cedar (*Cedrus atlantica* 'Glauca')
silk tassel bush (*Garrya elliptica*)
tree heather (*Erica arborea*)
lichen-covered twigs

Sundries

30 cm (12 in) foam wreath ring (the type that has polystyrene not plastic at the base)
birch stars for edging (optional)
hot melt glue gun
about 10 small shiny baubles
0.56 mm stub wires (to secure baubles)
kebab or cocktail sticks, or 0.90 mm wires (to secure candles)

Method

1. Using a hot melt glue gun (the adhesive is stronger and sets instantly, but be careful, because it will burn), attach the birch stars to the side of the wreath frame. Do not pre-soak the frame because the glue will not adhere readily. Overlap some of the stars slightly to conceal the foam. If you are using leaves instead, overlap them too.

2. Once the glue has set, place the ring in the sink and dribble small amounts of water on top of the exposed foam to soak lightly.

3. Cut all the foliage into short lengths of approximately 8 cm (3 in), ensuring there is a small amount of clean stem end to insert into the foam. Distribute these over the top of the foam on slight angles curving over the edge of the design as well as partially covering the surface. Use the *Garrya* tassels to slightly overhang the edge - their pendulous habit is ideally suited to this.

4. Cut the *Ornithogalum* stems to approximately 5 cm (2 in) lengths and place in the foam in a herringbone pattern (not in a straight line) through the design.

5. Insert a cocktail stick or heavy stub wire into the base of the candle to secure. You may need to hold the wax over a small flame to soften it slightly, so that the wire can be inserted.

6. Take a lighter 0.56 mm stub wire and thread it through the loop at the top of the bauble. Twist the wire ends together to secure. Place the candles and the baubles between the *Ornithogalum* flowers. If the baubles are small, group them together in clusters of two or three for impact.

7. Check for any visible gaps where the foam may be visible and fill in with the short foliage. Spray lightly with water.

Tips

- This design will last for several weeks if kept cool and sprayed; the *Ornithogalum* and foliage are long lasting.
- If the flower stems are difficult to insert into the foam, insert a 0.71 mm stub wire up through the stem to help insertion.

Alternative materials

Flowers – roses, spray carnations, *Bouvardia*, statice (*Limonium*), *Eustoma*.
Foliage – *Hebe* (small variety), ming fern (*Asparagus umbellatus*).

Door ring

Use

This ring, or wreath as it is also known, is used for decoration on the front door at Christmas time, and can also be adapted for interior use on the wall.

The classic door wreath is associated with Christmas in the UK, but in other European countries, such as Germany and Holland, they are often displayed at other times of the year as a sign of welcome. Traditionally, a wreath of holly was seen as a symbol of good fortune and from this, the evergreen door wreath has evolved.

Rings or wreaths dress a door effectively and are most commonly made from a mixture of evergreen foliage, including: box (*Buxus sempervirens*); berried ivy (*Hedera helix*); pines such as Scots pine (*Pinus sylvestris*); blue spruce (*Abies procera*); holly (*Ilex aquifolium*); and yew (*Taxus baccata*).

For decoration, fruits such as apples and cones are often added or, if it is to be used indoors, baubles and other glitzy adornments are popular.

Materials

Flowers and foliage

about 10 stems box (*Buxus sempervirens*)
10 x stems berried ivy (*Hedera helix*)
10 x stems blue spruce (*Abies procera*)
6 x dried lotus heads (*Nelumbo nucifera*)

Sundries

35 cm (14 in) wire wreath frame
about 8 large handfuls of *Sphagnum* moss
1 reel of 0.56 mm gauge reel mossing wire
1 reel of backing plastic (optional)
mossing pins
about 10 long 0.71 mm and 0.90 mm gauge stub wires (to attach cones, apples and cinnamon sticks)
a small amount of raffia (to tie cinnamon sticks)
1 m (3 ft 4 in) ribbon (optional)
cinnamon sticks

4

9–10

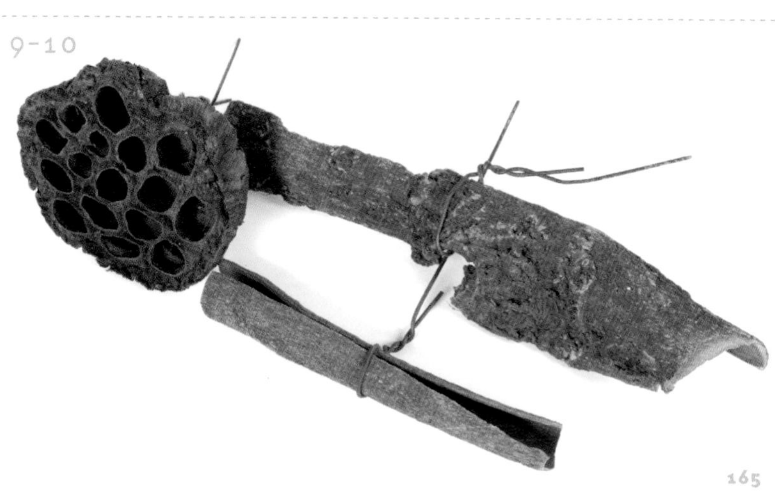

Method

1. Tease out the moss and remove any twigs or small stones. If the moss is very wet, you may need to squeeze it over a bucket to get rid of excess water.

2. Attach the end of the reel wire to the outside edge of the frame.

3. Make approximately 10 compact sausage shapes out of the moss, ensuring that it is compacted as much as possible. Place the first of these on the frame and bind on firmly with reel wire. Do this with all the other moss 'sausages' making them as compact as possible – this is very important, to ensure that the base is firm and secure for the wires to be inserted.

4. Cover the entire frame with moss. Cut off the reel wire and tuck the end under one of the first binds. Return the end back into the moss base.

5. Give the moss a quick trim to neaten it up. To secure a means of attachment to the door or wall, take a long stub wire (0.90 mm gauge) through the moss (ensuring it is under the wire frame) and bring the wires together flush to the frame. Join the two wire ends together to form a loop or leave open if it is to be attached to a door-knocker. This will not be visible, so it does not need to look attractive, but should be secure.

6. If you are attaching a protective backing, turn the frame over and pin a length of plastic wrap to the underside in a 'lapping' method. This can be quite time consuming, so a faster alternative is to pin large leaves such as cherry laurel (*Prunus laurocerasus*) onto the back of the frame. These do, however, dry out in a couple of days and can become detached from the moss.

7. The frame is now ready to decorate with evergreen foliage. Cut the foliage into short lengths, approximately 10 cm (4 in) long, and defoliate a small amount from the stem ends. Place small bunches of the same foliage type onto the frame and bind on with the mossing wire, as with the moss. One type of foliage may be used, but in the illustrated design, a combination of materials was used including *Buxus*, *Abies* and berried *Hedera*.

8. Bind each bunch firmly onto the moss frame in close order, so no gaps are visible. Once the frame is covered, add the final materials for decoration.

9. Prepare the lotus heads by taking a 0.71 mm gauge stub wire through the base of the seedhead and bringing the two wires down parallel with each other and the short stem. Twist one wire around the other and the stem to secure. This should form a double leg mount, which can then be inserted into the moss.

10. To prepare the cinnamon sticks, tie a few together with a flexible material like raffia, which will keep them securely together - unlike wire, which is not sufficiently secure. Take a medium gauge wire (0.56 or 0.71 mm) under the tied raffia and twist the two wires together underneath the sticks.

11. Distribute the cinnamon sticks evenly around the foliage wreath or in a pattern of your choice.

12. Finish with a bow (see page 191) and position either at the top or at the base of the wreath – whichever you prefer.

If exposed to damp conditions, this design will last for up to three weeks on the door; if placed inside, the foliage will start to dry out within four to five days.

Tips

- It is not always necessary to cover the back of the moss frame if it will not scratch the door.
- If the materials are lightweight, a double leg mount wire is sufficient. With heavy materials such as apples, a single leg mount will leave one wire long enough to be inserted right through the frame and returned back for extra security.

Alternative Materials

Foliage – *Pinus sylvestris, Juniperus, Cryptomeria, Cupressus.*

To decorate – preserved orange slices and walnuts.

Christmas swag

Use

Swags are timeless, traditional wall hangings that remain popular and have the advantage of not taking up valuable floor space. They are wonderful adornments for stairways, mantelpieces and galleries, or they can be adapted to hang straight on a wall.

Swags are constructed in the same way as a garland, but whereas the latter tends to be used to drape around a fixture - such as a church pillar or stairway - swags often hang vertically. They are usually shorter than garlands and are less flexible.

Made primarily with evergreen foliage, they are usually situated at eye level, so they give lots of impact. They are ideal for a variety of special occasions, but are usually associated with Christmas. For a natural festive look, they are decorated with fruit and nuts, or, for a glitzier air, they are adorned with baubles.

The following method can be adapted according to the size and quantity of materials being used. In summer, for instance, place large, blousy flowers such as peonies or roses in groups amongst the foliage; keep the blooms fresh by inserting their stems in plastic water phials. For even larger materials, it may be preferable to wire them together and insert them into a foundation of moss wrapped with chicken wire. The illustrated design, which teams an orange colour theme with natural birch (*Betula*) stars and gilded oak (*Quercus*) foliage, is made for Christmas. The foundation consists of a mix of evergreen foliage, which has a blue/grey colour and looks particularly good with orange because blue and orange are direct complementary colours (see page 22).

Materials

Flowers and foliage

15 x blue pine (*Abies procera*) cut into short lengths of 10 cm (4 in) maximum
gum (*Eucalyptus glaucescens*)
gold-sprayed oak (*Quercus*)
4 - 5 x preserved whole oranges
25 x slices of preserved orange (used in groups of 3 wired together)
21 x birch (*Betula pendula*) twigs (short stems)

Sundries

2 m (7 ft) length of medium-thickness rope
0.56 mm gauge reel (mossing wire)
5 x orange baubles
3 x large birch (*Betula*) stars
1 m (40 in) gold ribbon (for the bow)
0.71 mm and 0.90 mm stub wires (for support wiring orange slices and baubles)

Alternative materials

Scots pine (*Pinus sylvestris*), box (*Buxus sempervirens*), strawberry tree (*Arbutus unedo*), apples and cinnamon sticks.

Tips

- It is not advisable to use hydrangeas in early summer when they often wilt. They are better to use in late summer and early autumn when they naturally dry in situ.
- Bushier foliage like pine fills out more quickly and its flat form gives a perfect backdrop to winter swags. You will need about five stems of *Eucalyptus* to achieve a similar volume.

Method

1. Cut the *Eucalyptus* and pine foliage into short lengths – approximately 10 cm (4 in) long. Do the same with the gold oak and place them all in their own piles ready to attach to the rope with the reel wire.

2. Prepare the orange slices by placing three together, one on top of the other. Take a 0.71 mm gauge stub wire and insert through the outer segments as near to the rind as possible. Twist the ends of the wire together, as close as possible to the outer rind. This creates a wired end, which will bind onto the rope.

3. With a 0.90 mm stub wire, pierce one of the slits in the whole dried oranges. Again, bring the two ends of the wire together and twist at the base to secure.

4. Skewer a small hole into the bark of the birch stars with a kebab stick or metal skewer. Insert a 0.90 mm gauge wire through the bark, then bring the wire ends together and twist. The heavier the material, the heavier the wire should be to support them.

5. To make the bow, follow the instructions on page191.

6. Now that all the materials are prepared, take the end of the rope and attach the reel wire. Do this by binding a length of the wire several times, and as firmly as possible, around the top of the rope. You should also create a small loop with which to hang the swag. Secure with further binds of wire.

7. Take the first two or three stems of pine and bind its tips onto the rope a few centimetres from the end of the stem. If you are using a bow, it can be added at this stage.

8. Add a couple of bunches of *Eucalyptus* so that a pattern of evenly distributed material begins. Take some of the decorative items, such as a baubles or oranges, and bind in on top of the foliage. Successive bunches of foliage will help to secure the materials, so do not worry if the items seem a little insecure initially.

9. Add more pine, then some of the gilded oak: the gold will give a welcome break of colour. The first of the three birch stars could go in along with a group of orange slices. Once you have bound one of each item onto the rope, repeat the pattern until approximately 10 cm (4 in) before the end of the rope.

10. To finish the swag - and maintain the same visual direction of materials - attach some foliage to the bottom end of the rope in the opposite direction (with the tips of the foliage facing downwards). This ensures that the ends of the swag are finished.

11. Cut the binding wire leaving enough to take under a previous bind. Pull firmly to secure and insert the end of the wire into the foliage so the sharp end is not exposed.

12. If hung in a cool place, the swag will last well for up to three weeks. The decorative items can be kept and stored until needed again.

2

3

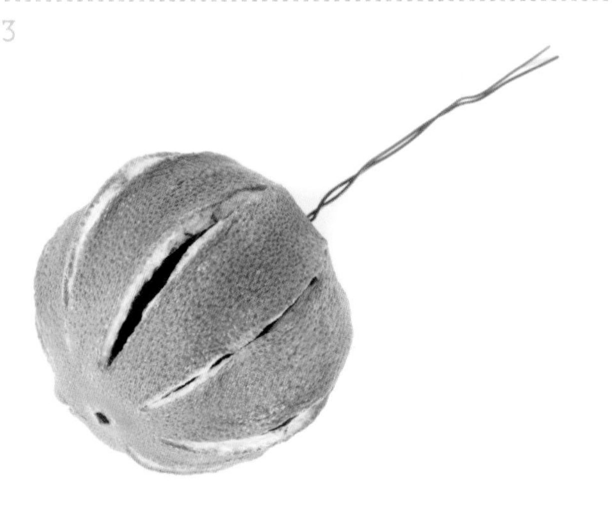

Buffet table arrangement

Use

This long, slim arrangement would also be suitable for a top table at a wedding, a speaker's table at a function, or to decorate a mantelpiece.

This type of arrangement is designed to cascade over the front of the table or mantelpiece. The choice of flowers and foliage is therefore important, because some hanging, or curved materials are needed to achieve the cascading effect.

Table flowers can be enhanced with the inclusion of fruits. These are often heavy and need to be securely inserted. Make sure that they will not exude excessive juice, which would stain a tablecloth.

It is always wise to check the space you have been allocated for a table design at a venue. Once all the crockery is in place, this can often be less than you think. It is important to check that the flower materials are free of pests and diseases as they will be viewed close-up at the table. Avoid any irritant plant materials like *Euphorbia* and *Aconitum*. Stamens from lilies should be removed.

This design uses the late spring foliage Soloman's seal (*Polygonatum*). It has a useful natural curve and appears quite bold when viewed from a distance. This has been interspersed with ivy (*Hedera helix*) to convey a natural flowing appearance. The focal flowers need to have impact and the pink *Paeonia* give depth and wow factor to the centre.

Materials

Flowers and foliage

10 x *Paeonia*
10 x *Ageratum*
10 x snapdragon (*Antirrhinum majus*)
10 x lady's mantle (*Alchemilla mollis*)
10 x sweet pea (*Lathyrus odoratus*)
10 x pink roses
10 x Soloman's seal (*Polygonatum*)
about 15 ivy trails (*Hedera helix*)
Cotinus

Sundries

1 plastic tray about 60 cm (24 in) in length that will hold two bricks of foam lengthways
2 x bricks of florists' foam (wet)
pot tape to secure
florists' scissors and knife

2

3

Method

1. Soak the foam and place it on its edge in the tray. This is important, because you will need to push the stems up into the foam to achieve a downwards flowing appearance. Wrap pot tape around each brick and pull firmly to secure.

2. Position *Polygonatum* at the front of the design and intersperse with ivy trails. It is important to place some shorter materials at the back of the design to give actual balance, or the design could topple forwards. Once you have established the foliage outline, place the focal flowers low down, close to the foam. Some should be at slightly different angles and levels to avoid a uniform line.

3. Add some of the smaller transitional materials such as the *Antirrhinum*. Place them on the outer edges first to define the shape, and save one or two shorter stems for the centre. As these designs tend to be horizontal in shape, it is easier and more effective to simply distribute materials across the whole of the design in a herringbone pattern rather than in a uniform line.

4. Fill in the design with the remaining materials - but without overcrowding. Remember to keep the stems of the lighter materials longer, and to recess those that are visually heavier. Ensure there is also interest and impact at the back of the design, because it will also be on view – particularly on a top table at a wedding.

Tips

- Ensure some of the front materials are arching or trailing to give a flowing appearance when the design is placed on the table.
- At dinner tables, do not use materials that are an irritant or highly scented.
- Avoid using berries that may be attractive to children and also stain the tablecloths.
- Table arrangements are seen at close quarters, so they must be finished to a high standard – remove any damaged or diseased foliage.

Alternative materials

Focal flowers - Asiatic or oriental lilies, sunflowers (*Helianthus*), large roses, *Chrysanthemum* 'Shamrock' or *Chrysanthemum* 'Anastasia', *Anthurium, Gerbera, Dahlia.*

Transitional flowers - Veronica (*Hebe*), statice (*Limonium*), *Freesia, Dianthus* spray, *Anigozanthus, Crocosmia,* larkspur, *Scabiosa, Sandersonia.*

Foliage - soft ruscus (*Danae racemosa*) is ideal due to its arching form, ladder fern (*Nephrolepis*).

chapter 10

Design work

Once the essential building blocks have been mastered, design skills can be developed further by adaptation and experimentation.

However, you cannot know when to break the rules successfully unless you know what those rules are.

The last 30 years have seen great advancements in floral design and Europe has been at the forefront of this development. Each country has its own leading lights in floristry design, who have done much to emphasise the professionalism of the industry through their training.

Many floral designs can be recognised as being influenced by a particular designer's style, or country of origin. Their inspiration and creativity is often drawn from other parts of the art world - such as architecture, textiles, interior design or furniture design. One of the great pleasures of floristry is that it explores and creates using all of nature's materials. These, in turn, are constantly changing and providing new opportunities to experiment.

Floristry is no longer just about flowers – it features structures, constructions and techniques, which use weird and wonderful plant materials and exciting accessories.

Urn of peonies

Use

This would be ideal for a simple summer dinner party, placed on a buffet or side table, or at a wedding.

Some flowers almost demand to be used in a certain way. The beauty of these two varieties of peony is enhanced by simply massing them together and adding just a few trails of ivy (*Hedera helix*). The pleasantly distressed urn is a perfect, classic shape and the whole composition works.

Porous containers, such as terracotta, should first be lined with plastic or Cellophane before filling with foam. In this design, the foam is not very high above the container since a relatively low arrangement was required.

Tip

Sphagnum moss or scrunched Cellophane can be used as packing instead of off-cuts of foam.

Alternative material

This round, massed arrangement needs dominant rounded flowers, not flat, saucer-like blooms.

Flowers – large roses such as *R. 'Esperance'* (pink), *R. 'Sphinx'* (yellow), *R. 'Sweet Avalanche'* (peach), *R. 'Avalanche'* (white), *R. 'Grand prix'* (dark red), *Hydrangea*, or *Dianthus*.

Foliage – jasmine (*Jasminum*), periwinkle (*Vinca*).

Materials

Flowers and foliage

8 x pale pink *Paeonia*
8 x dark pink *Paeonia*
5 x ivy (*Hedera helix*) trails
5 x guelder rose (*Viburnam opulus*)

Sundries

urn - this one is 20 cm (8 in) tall
Cellophane to line container
1 brick of florists' foam

2

Method

1. Line the container if necessary. Soak the foam, then cut to size and place in the container. Use any off-cuts to pack into the sides to ensure the foam remains secure.

2. Place a group of ivy trails to one side of the urn – ensure these are firmly inserted.

3. Begin to arrange the peonies. Start on the outer edge of one side and gradually build up into the centre. There should be a gentle profile, meaning that the central flowers should be slightly taller than the outer ones.

4. Ensure that the mechanics are hidden on the edge of the design by placing the outer peonies sufficiently low over the rim.

5. Add the *Viburnum opulus*. If possible, cut on the older, brown wood which takes up water quicker than the newer secondary stems. Spray lightly with water and keep away from direct sunlight.

3

4

Spring design with a structure

Use

This design has a contemporary feel, and would be appropriate for a modern hotel foyer or office.

The soft, tactile buds of *Salix caprea* and the branches of *Cornus alba* are both synonymous with spring and work well when used with rich-coloured anemones.

When twig structures are used, it is preferable to restrict the different types of the plant material, and to highlight the beauty of a specific flower - such as the anemones used here.

Fashioning the *Cornus* into an archway gives a decorative touch, yet the seasonal compatibility of the materials is very natural and vegetative (see page 190).

Containers should always be suitably sympathetic and preferably not predominant. The purple colour creates a partially monochromatic colour combination when used with the cerise anemones. The wicker weave adds to the natural theme.

Materials

Flowers and foliage

20 x pink *Anemone caerula*
10 x *Cornus alba* 'Kesselringii'
5 x pussy willow (*Salix caprea*)
reindeer moss to cover the foam

Sundries

shallow wicker container with a loose weave
1 brick of florists' foam
0.71 mm gauge stub wires (to pin on the moss)

Tips

- If the soft *Anemone* stems will not insert easily into the foam, use a florists' knife, or thin piece of cane to make a hole. Some longer anemones may benefit from an internal support wire using 0.71 mm stub wire.
- Only use fresh *Cornus* and *Salix* which are flexible.
- To keep anemones fresh for longer, insert water phials into the foam or attach to the twigs. Place the *Anemone* stems into these.

Alternative materials

Flowers - *Tulipa, Craspedia, Ranunculus, Freesia, Crocosmia.*

Twigs - birch (*Betula*), dogwood (*Cornus*).

Method

1. Soak the foam and cut to the shape of the container. It should not exceed the height of the container and should preferably be a little lower. Ensure that the stability of the plant materials is not compromised. If the container is not watertight, line it with plastic or Cellophane prior to inserting the foam.

2. Insert the ends of the *Cornus* into the foam through the holes in the sides of the container. If your container is solid, cut foam that is higher than the rim of the container and place the stem ends in the foam.

3. Bend the tips of the *Cornus* over to the other side of the container and insert these into the foam.

4. Repeat with the *Salix*, interspersing them between the *Cornus* until an archway effect is created the length of the container.

5. Gently insert the *Anemone* stem ends into the foam leaving some as long as possible to give height above the structure.

6. Finally, pin moss onto any visible foam using 0.71 mm gauge stub wire, bent into hairpins.

4

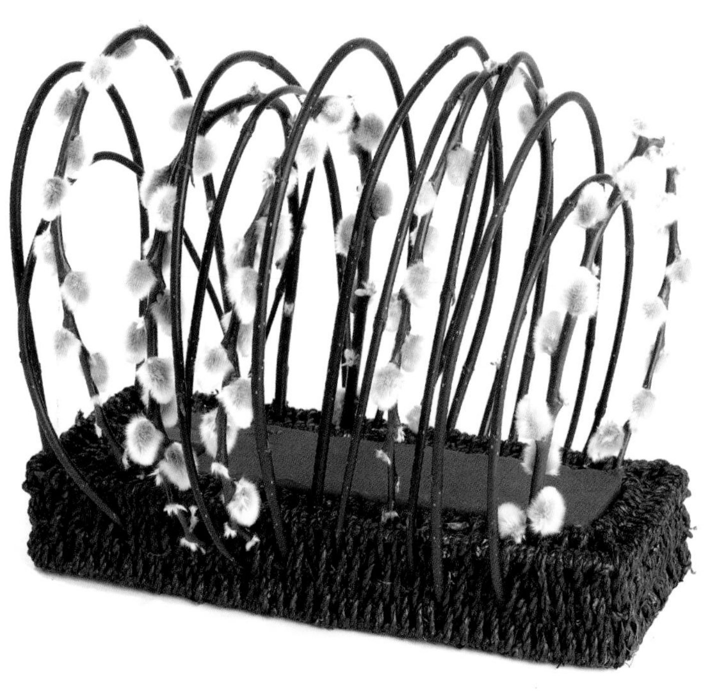

Spring vegetative arrangement

Use

This is an ideal design for spring flowers, which are well suited to this naturalistic style. It would work well on a reception desk or against a wall.

'Vegetative style' simply means using plant material as it would naturally grow and in its natural season. For instance, winter materials would not be used with summer ones; and ground cover plants, such as *Rubus* or periwinkle (*Vinca*), would be used horizontally as they naturally grow. The spring flowers in this design are placed vertically and in small groups. The bare, twisted branches of the *Corylus* are sympathetically seasonal and the moss provides an unobtrusive ground cover material to conceal the mechanics.

The oblong shape of this design is often used for vegetative styles, though round or square designs work equally well. The complementary yellow of the *Ranunculus* with the blue of the hyacinths is vibrant and refreshing.

Materials

Flowers and foliage

12 - 14 x *Hyacinthus*
about 8 *Ranunculus*
about 6 stems cork-screw hazel
Corylus avellana 'Contorta'
7 x *Ornithogalum dubium*
1 strong branch
about 7 twigs of willow or similar

Sundries

shallow, oblong container approximately 30 cm (12 in) long
plastic or Cellophane to line container (if not using ceramic or plastic)
1 brick of florists' foam
0.71 mm gauge green wires cut into hairpins (to pin the moss)
6 x heavy guage wires, garden canes, or kebab sticks

Method

1. Prepare the mechanics by soaking a brick of foam. Pin holders could also be used, though you would need four large ones for a long container similar to the one illustrated.

2. Place the foam into the container ensuring that you have cut it level to the surface of the container as most stems are used upright rather than angled. If you are using a metal container, as illustrated, ensure it is lined with Cellophane or plastic before the foam is added, because the side seams are not always watertight.

3. Begin by positioning the branch over your container horizontally. Place the twigs vertically, working from the back forwards to the front.

4. Position the taller *Ranunculus* flowers in front of the hazel and stagger in height slightly. Place these in two or three groups along the foam – depending on the length of the container.

5. Prepare the hyacinths by inserting a strong wire up inside the stem, or even a thin garden cane, or a kebab stick.

6. Place the shorter hyacinths at the front – again, in groups of two or three.

7. When you have positioned all the flowers, place the moss over the flowers, place the moss over the foam and between the stems. Secure by pinning the moss with hairpins made from lengths of stub wire cut into short lengths and bent into a simple 'U' shape.

3

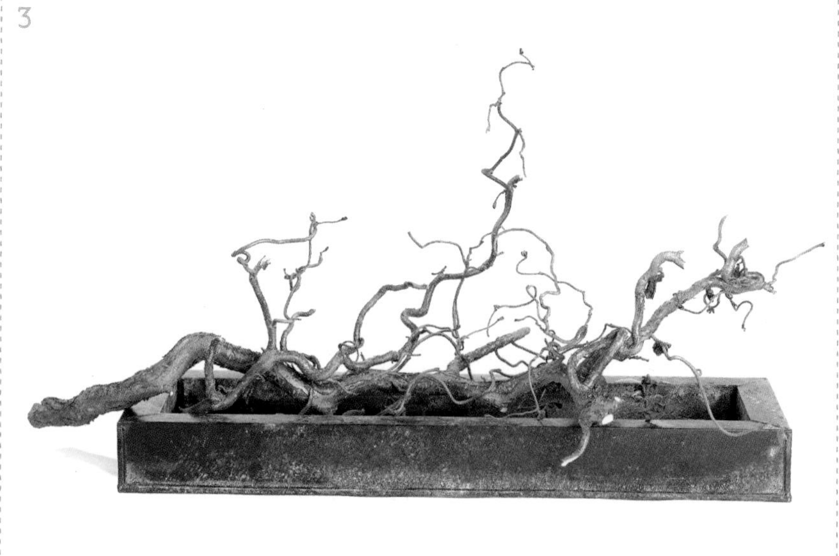

Tips

- If the soft stems will not insert easily into the foam, make a small hole in the foam with a florists' knife before placing the stems; this is particularly necessary for the *Hyacinth*.

- Pebbles would also work as a ground cover instead of moss.

- Hyacinths can also be used with their bulbs; this gives a different form and the flower usually lasts longer this way. Simply clean off the soil from the roots and pin the base into the foam using strong stub wire.

Alternative flowers

Autumn – *Dahlia, Crocosmia*, red hot pokers (*Kniphofia*), dogwood (*Cornus*) stripped of leaves. *Rudbeckia* seedheads, lotus (*Nelumbo nucifera*) seedheads.

Summer – Veronica (*Hebe*), roses, Larkspur, poppy (*Papaver*) seedheads.

Spring - *Narcissus, Muscari, Anemone, Tulipa.*

Winter - *Chrysanthemum.*

Design using a birch bowl

Use

This design is ideal as a table centre for a special occasion.

Spring flowers are loved for their prettiness, and often their scent. They are, however, often shorter-lived than other cut flowers and as such are best placed directly in water rather than foam.

This design uses a plastic bowl (placed inside the pre-formed log bowl) and scrunched chicken wire to hold the stems in place. Chicken wire is a traditional alternative medium to foam. In the climate of re-cycling and sustainability, it represents a useful alternative to foam.

Materials

Flowers and foliage

20 - 25 x tulips (*Tulipa*)

12 - 15 x hyacinths (*Hyacinthus*)

box *Buxus sempervirens*

birch *Betula pendula* twigs

moss

Sundries

plastic bowl

1 m^2 (3 ½ ft^2) chicken wire

reel wire

wire cutters

florists' scissors

pre-formed long bowl

2

3

Method

1. Prepare the container by scrunching up the chicken wire, but not too tightly. Fill the bowl with water.

2. Place the scrunched wire into the bowl and secure by attaching a length of reel wire to one side. Take the reel wire underneath the bowl and attach it to the opposite side. Repeat on the opposite side for extra security.

3. Remove the lower leaves from the tulips and hyacinths. Cut the material destined for the centre of the design to a length of approximately 20 cm (8 in) higher than the container; and cut the material for the outer edges slightly shorter. This will create a domed profile.

4. Place flowers within the circular outline, distributing them evenly, until the design looks full.

Tips

- Use large, flexible chicken wire, or the holes will be too small for the stems to slot through.

- Do not be put off by the haphazard appearance of the first few stem placements. It will improve dramatically as more stems are placed.

Alternative flowers and foliage

Roses, *Bouvardia*, *Matricaria*, veronica (*Hebe*), sweet peas (*Lathyrus*), *Freesia*.

Acknowledgements

Most of the photographs in this book are by Toby Smith (**www.tobysmith.com**) and Oliver Gordon (**www.olivergordon.co.uk**). Our thanks to them for their care and precision.

We would also like to thank the other photographers for their generous contributions, especially: Chris Allerton (pages 102, 103; **www.chrisallerton.com**); Judith Blacklock (pages 10, 59, 62, 125); Jonny Draper (pages 30, 42, 60, 78, 148; **www.jonnydraper.co.uk**); Katya Eliseeva (pages 8, 9, 21, 23, 28, 60, 61,104, 146,147); Sophie Gordon (book cover; **www.theunseenworld.co.uk**); International Flower Bulb Bureau (pages 25, 27, 29,174); Ash Mills (page 7; **www.AshMills.com**); William Ohl (pages 17, 50, 51, 127 - 129; **www.ohlphotography.com**).

The following designers have also added their work to the book: Rose Edge (page 30); Sherree Francis (book cover); Hazel Harris (pages 102, 103); Dawn Jennings (page 59); Sergey Malyuchenko (pages 8, 9, 21, 23, 28, 60, 61,104, 146, 147; **http://de-bloemist.narod.ru**); Susan McManus (page 60); Lindsay Richards (page 125); Jane Thompson (page 148); and Catherine Vickers (pages 42, 78). We owe much gratitude to David Winston of Winston Flowers in Boston for arranging for some of his team's fine design work to be photographed for the book (pages 17, 50, 51, 127 - 129; **www.winstonflowers.com**).

Many thanks to Laura Leong (**ljleong1@yahoo.co.uk**) for producing all of the line drawings so swiftly and effectively and for understanding what was required.

The team at the flower school - Georgina Goldsmith, Tomoko Godfrey, Tom Koson and Lindsay Richards - gets our big appreciation for its fine work in preparing the flowers, acting as models, editing, ordering pizzas and lots more. Many thanks also to Jacqueline Edwards.

Dr Christina Curtis has been impressive - as always - with her amazing knowledge of botanical nomenclature.

And lastly, thank you to Claire Hawkes at SCW Design for her enthusiasm and excellent design skills. Her calmness and good spirits under pressure made this book possible.

Designed by SCW Design (**www.scw.uk.com**).

The beautiful flowers were supplied by Metz (**www.metz.com**).

Glossary

Basing – the use of materials so as to form a closed, uniform surface with no space in between.

Binding point – the point at which a wired design (such as a bridal bouquet, corsage, posy or handtied) is bound to secure all the stems (wired or natural) together.

Bullion wire – a fine gauge (usually 0.28 mm) decorative wire, slightly wavy in appearance, used for decorative detailing in wired designs. It is available in an assortment of different colours and would not normally be hidden.

Chicken wire – a mesh wire with holes of varying sizes and gauges. It is often used as a means of reinforcing large-scale designs (to protect foam from crumbling), or as a medium for securing heavy materials.

Floral foam – a lightweight water-retaining medium, which is used to secure stems. It is available for fresh flowers (green colour) and will retain water when soaked; alternatively, it is available for dry or artificial flowers (in pale brown or grey). The most widely available shape is a rectangular brick measuring 20 cm (8 in) in length. It is also manufactured in small cylinders and much larger blocks for large-scale designs. Rainbow® foam is manufactured in a variety of colours. It needs to be soaked for longer and needs additional food, eg. Chrysal. It supports and is also decorative and not meant to be hidden.

Focal flowers – usually the largest and most dominant flowers within a design, which attract the viewing eye and form a focal area / area of interest

Impactive – dominance through colour or form. It draws attention to a focal area.

'Lazy S' - In traditional floristry designs, flowers are often placed through the centre in the pattern of an 'S'. Another word for Hogarth curve.

Le Bump® – small dome-shaped piece of foam encased in a green plastic cage. It is mainly used as an attachment to the top of a funeral base in order to assemble a spray. It can also be employed on screens made of metal mesh for contemporary work.

Moss – a natural plant material that grows on the ground – often in damp shady conditions.

- ***Sphagnum* moss** – used for covering wire frames at Christmas, it forms a very sturdy medium and allows insertion of heavy materials such as fruit. It is pale brown / green / reddish in colour and has a woolly texture.
- **Reindeer moss (*Cladonia rangiferina*)**– as the name implies it is associated with reindeers and forms part of their diet. It is imported from Norway and its natural colour is a pale grey. However, it is also dyed in other colours such as pale pink, purple, terracotta and orange. It is primarily used as a decorative ground cover in floristry designs.
- **Bun moss (*Leucobryum glaucum*)** – purchased in small crates, this moss has a lovely velvety appearance like small green hummocks. It is harvested in the UK mainly from the New Forest but can also be imported. To keep fresh it should be sprayed regularly and allowed some light to keep its green colour. Used as a decorative ground cover, the top of the moss is its best feature. It's quite thick in depth and often needs the underside trimming down to be useable.
- **Carpet (flat) moss** – much flatter than bun moss and a rougher textural appearance. Ideal for a surface dressing on planted bowls and in European vegetative designs.
- **Spanish moss (*Tillandsia*)** – this 'moss' is actually an air plant and is very stringy in appearance with a pale grey colour. It works well when used in a trailing habit for softening designs and adding interest.

Mount wiring – this creates a false stem so that a flower or foliage can be inserted into the binding point of a bouquet or anchored into a medium such as foam or moss.

Pinholder – a small, circular lead weighted metal base with sharp needle-like protrusions into which to secure flower stems. It is particularly good for spring flowers, as the pinholder allows for the direct uptake of water.

Recessing – the placement of materials at a lower level, designed to force the eye to move into a design giving depth and creating extra interest.

Reel wire – available both as functional reel wires to secure wired stems together or a range of different materials from twiggy structures to binding moss. It is also available in many different colours.

Stay wire – this refers to the taping of another wire onto an already wired flower in order to make it stronger or longer. It is often a gauge higher than the original wire used.

Stitch wiring – this wiring method is used to support individual leaves such as ivy leaves for inclusion in small, wired designs such as a corsage.

Stub wire – a pre-cut length of wire available in several different gauges used for supporting and controlling flowers and other materials. It is widely available in 18 cm (7.5 in) or 24 cm (10 in) lengths.

Support wiring – a means of strengthening and manipulating stems. It is primarily used in wedding designs but also in some funeral work where tributes are handled several times. Once wired, stems should have a degree of natural movement.

Transitional flowers – small to medium sized flowers that are used in mixed designs to complement the bolder focal flowers. They help to fill out the shape of the overall design.

Vegetative – the use of plant materials as they would grow naturally and in their natural season. For instance, groundcover plants such as *Rubus tricolor* and *Hedera* would be used horizontally as they grow. Conversely *Iris* or *Narcissi* would be placed vertically and in small clumps.

Techniques

Using foam

Wet foam should be placed in water that is deeper than the piece of foam being soaked. It should never be pushed down under the water because this could cause air blockages and prevent the foam from soaking fully. It should take approximately one minute to soak a conventional brick - or until the air bubbles cease. When ready, the foam will be level with the water and the colour will have changed from light to dark green. Larger pieces, made from a heavier density foam and Rainbow® foam, take longer to soak.

Making a bow

1. Take approximately 2 m (6 ½ ft) of ribbon and cross the tip of one end over the longer length and place on a horizontal angle to the vertical length. This will create one of the tails, so ensure it is the length you want. Hold the point where the two lengths cross between your fingers – this will form the centre of the bow. Do not let go as you progress.
2. Now take the longer length and fold into the centre, ensuring that a second loop is formed the same size as the first one. There should now be a figure of eight shape.
3. Take the long length once again, and this time fold behind the loops to form the third loop, still holding in the centre.
4. Fold the final length of ribbon into the centre to make the fourth and final loop. Secure by tying the centre with a seperate length of ribbon. Trim a 'V' into the tail ends, or cut on an angle to finish.

Chamfering

This refers to the slight shaving of the edge of foam to soften the square edge. It is often done on blocks of foam and on some foam funeral bases to facilitate basing / stem coverage.

Using chicken wire

When using as protection to prevent foam crumbling (as with large arrangements), simply place over the foam and insert the ends of the wire into the foam and down the inside of the container. If using as a medium in which to secure stems, scrunch up into a slightly domed shape to fit the container. Secure a piece of fine silver reel wire (0.32 mm gauge) to one side of the chicken wire, take underneath the container, and attach to the chicken wire on the opposite side. Repeat this process on the other corner. This will ensure that the chicken wire is secured into the container.

Using knives

A knife should be used by gripping the handle, with all four fingers, and curling the thumb out of the way to prevent cuts. The movement should be swift and deft - this comes with practice. It is by far the best practice to use a knife when cutting materials, but this is not always possible for harder, woodier stems, or when cutting a large quantity.

Using foam

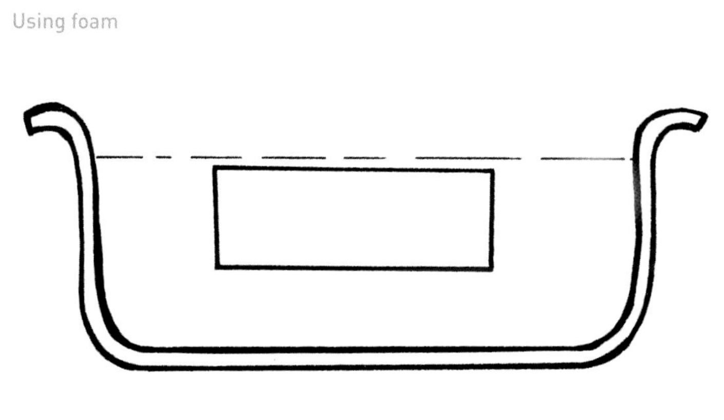

Chamfering

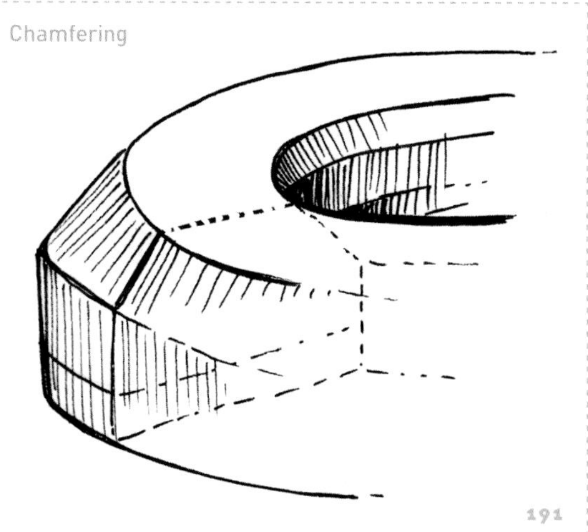

Pleating ribbon

1. Prepare the ribbon pleat by folding the ribbon, then bringing in another pleat to meet it. The whole pleat should be no wider than 5 cm (2 in), so each half pleat is approximately 2.5 cm (1 in).

2. Repeat this process until you have sufficient length to edge the frame outside and inside.

Pot tape (anchor tape)

The tape needs to be taken over the foam and pulled taut. It should be stuck securely to the sides of the container – for extra security, an additional short piece of tape can be placed across the original tape end, near the rim of the container so as to be less visible. Take care to avoid the very centre if using a large focal flower or candle.

Conditioning

Conditioning is the preparation of plant material before use, so that it will take up water and survive. This is essential as all stem ends seal if out of water for even a short time. To allow the maximum supply of water to enter the stem, cut it cleanly at a sharp angle with a clean, sharp knife or scissors. Remove about 10 % of the stem length. Any foliage that would lie below the water line or that might enter the foam should also be removed. The stem should then be immediately placed in fresh, tepid water in a clean vessel.

Add cut flower food to the water, following the instructions on the sachet. Wholesalers sell proprietary products in large tins or dispensers and it is economical to purchase cut flower food this way. Cut flower food allows the flowers to mature fully and last longer. Spraying also helps to keep plant material fresh.

Mature foliage can be left under water for an hour or so as it also takes up water through the leaves. Do not treat immature and grey foliage in this way as it quickly becomes waterlogged.

Never hammer or smash the stems as this encourages rapid bacterial growth.

Pleating ribbon

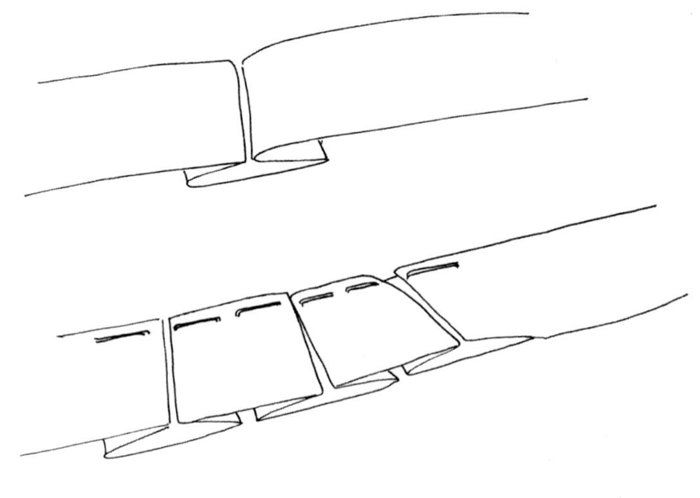

Pot tape

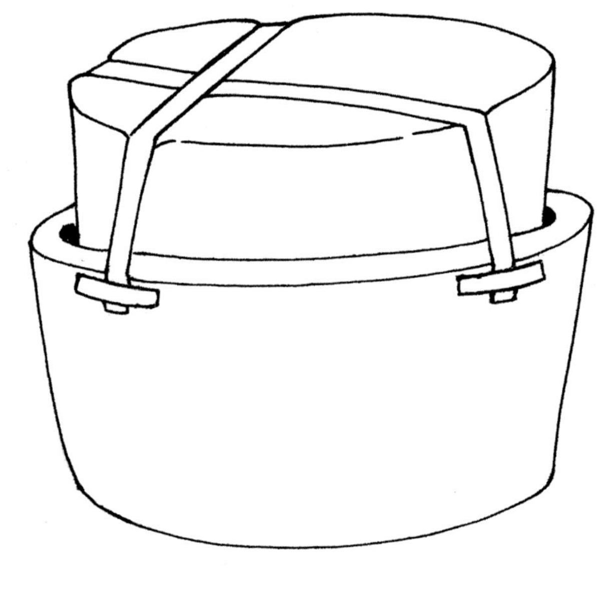